WINTER SUN

CHINESE LITERATURE TODAY BOOK SERIES

WINTER SUN

POEMS

Shi Zhi

Translated by Jonathan Stalling
Introduction by Zhang Qinghua

UNIVERSITY OF OKLAHOMA PRESS : NORMAN

This book is published with the generous assistance of China's National Office for Teaching Chinese as a Foreign Language, Beijing Normal University's College of Chinese Language and Literature, the University of Oklahoma's College of Arts and Sciences, and *World Literature Today* magazine.

Library of Congress Cataloging-in-Publication Data

Zhi, Shi.
  Winter sun : poems / Shi Zhi ; translated by Jonathan Stalling ; introduction by Zhang Qinghua.
    p. cm. — (Chinese literature today book series ; v. 1)
  Poems in Chinese with English translations.
  ISBN 978-0-8061-4241-8 (pbk. : alk. paper)
  I. Stalling, Jonathan. II. Title.
  PL2929.9.Z4.W56 2012
  895.1'152—dc23
              2011029726

Winter Sun: Poems is Volume 1 in the Chinese Literature Today Book Series.

1 2 3 4 5 6 7 8 9 10

 # CONTENTS

INTRODUCTION

THE RETURN OF THE PIONEER

Zhang Qinghua

多少不眠夜中忍受着疾病的折磨
在孤独冷漠中怀着诗意的憧憬
思想的婴儿经受了分娩的苦痛
终于喊出了惊天动地的哭声……

—食指,《啊, 尼采》

Through so many sleepless nights, he endured the torture of disease
Yet nurtured the poetic longing of solitude and indifference
An infant thought undergoes the trauma of birth
To finally cry out in an earth-shattering voice

—Shi Zhi, "Oh, Nietzsche"

Through the historical twists and turns of contemporary Chinese poetry, there is one person who cannot be ignored: that person is Shi Zhi 食指.

In 1968, two years into China's Cultural Revolution, the entire country was succumbing to red-hot revolutionary passions and national turmoil as everyone lost all sense of time, space, and individuality. It was then that two poems, written by a twenty-year-old, spread north and south of the Yangtze River through word of mouth and secret handwritten notes. These poems gave a voice to the common aspirations and faith of a generation of depressed youth. "This Is Beijing at 4:08" and "Believe in the Future" were written by Shi Zhi, who was then known as Guo Lusheng 郭路生, a name that means "born on the side of the Guo road."

This narrative has inevitably taken on mythological dimensions, and there are some who might question whether a twenty-year-old could have been so conscious of history as it unfolded, or who might raise the question of whether he was something of a political prophet. Perhaps he was not: perhaps all history comes about by chance; perhaps the narrative simply reflects a young man's cathartic articulation of his desperation. History may be only an aggregate of coincidences; yet these poems are powerful evidence that this tumultuous period in China's history was not all darkness and desolation. This alone is sufficiently important—that a poet can have a profound impact on history.

Guo Lusheng thus embarked upon his long, rich destiny—his life of poetry. In fact, however, he had begun writing as early as 1965. His early poems were imbued with a sentimental atmosphere full of youthful spirit and struggle, culminating in his early masterpiece "Ocean Trilogy" in 1967 and the more famous long poem "Fish Trilogy." In these two poems, he expressed his continually shifting feelings toward faith and doubt, joy and sadness, purity and despair, failure and renewal; those tensions energized his early writing with the most primal and important themes. The voice of this rebellious poet, who was increasingly burdened by mounting waves of depression, seized the spirit of his generation, who came to feel a collective, long-term resonance with his work. As his name spread like wildfire among his contemporaries, his works became a shelter throughout the Red Era. They have endured as immortal songs of life filled with an authentic spirit of witness to China's history.

In the decade between 1968 and 1978, Guo Lusheng was forced to undergo "rustication" or "reeducation" in the countryside at Xinghua Cun in Shanxi Province, and at his ancestral home in Yutai County, Shandong Province. In 1971 he joined the army, after which he began to suffer from clinical depression. He was later released from military service, and he returned to Beijing to seek long-term treatment for schizophrenia. During this time he also took two trips to Henan Province, where he was robbed and forced to live on the street, which only worsened his illness. In 1978 he wrote another masterpiece, "Mad Dog," at which time he gave himself the name "Shi Zhi" 食指, meaning "index finger," in response to the unwarranted social pressures distilled into the image of people pointing at his back.

In December 1978, the now-legendary underground poetry magazine *Jintian* 今天 (Today)—founded by the poets Bei Dao 北岛 and Mang Ke 芒克—began to publish modern Chinese poetry. The first issue included nine poems by Shi Zhi: "Believe in the Future," "Destiny," "Mad Dog," "Fish Trilogy," "This Is Beijing at 4:08," "Smoke," "It Would Be Best to Simply Forget Her," "Wine," and "Fury." Even by today's criteria, these poems have not only strong intellectual content and spiritual depth, but also a highly realized aesthetic quality. Nevertheless, they did not make him a national sensation alongside the Misty Poets—Bei Dao, Shu Ting 舒婷, Gu Cheng 顾城, Jiang He 江河, and others; instead, the poems were drowned out by the fiery waves of political and poetic polemics that surrounded the birth of the Misty Poetry movement.

The 1980s were a relatively calm period for Shi Zhi, and his poetry shifted from themes of youthful rebellion to a deeply introverted pathos. In 1975 he married Li Yalan 李雅兰 (they divorced in 1982), the Eurasian daughter of Li Lisan 李立三, the former leader of the Communist Party of China. Li Lisan held a high-level position in the central government after the founding of the People's Republic of China in 1949, yet he was persecuted to death during the Cultural Revolution in 1967. After the turbulent events of this short marriage, Shi Zhi entered middle age, and his work shifted again, toward a deeply felt grief. Because his elderly parents were no longer able to look after him, in 1990 he moved to the Beijing No. 3 Welfare House, an insane asylum. The harsh life and austere environment there forced him to think deeply about life, leading to some of his most moving poems. "In the Asylum," "My Destination," "When You Are Old," and "This Is How I Write My Songs" are the poems that best represent this period. Fortunately, after a decade of forgetfulness, the value of Shi Zhi's poetry was recognized again in Chinese poetic circles. Once scholars took stock of contemporary literary history, they came to acknowledge Shi Zhi as a spiritual guide with lasting artistic appeal. He quickly became the brightest star of the group known as the "buried Chinese poets," once again entering the public spotlight.

Yet despite his growing fame, Shi Zhi remained at the Beijing No. 3 Welfare House until 2002, when a woman named Zhai Hanle 翟寒乐 was able to get him released. She had fallen in love with his poems several years earlier and had begun to visit him frequently. As their emotional ties grew stronger, they realized that they could no longer bear to be separated from each other. After Shi Zhi left the welfare house, they created a home together. The long-suffering poet finally returned to an ordinary life; after a tumultuous ride, he can now enjoy his remaining years. From his more recent poems, such as "Autumn Sun" and "Sunlight of Winter," we can sense his calm and stable mind and genuinely appreciate his deep satisfaction and happiness.

SHI ZHI AS WITNESS: POETIC THEMES

In hindsight, the events of Shi Zhi's life are like a dramatic historical allegory arranged by fate. An examination of his poetry—from "Believe in the Future" in his twenties, to "Love Life" in his thirties, to "A Heartbroken Memory" in his forties, to "To Leap over the Gorge of Spiritual Death" in his fifties, and finally to "Oh, Nietzsche" in his sixties—reveals that his life has been filled with spiritual suffering, trials, and legends, which have proved to be a cold, yet radiant, blessing of fate. This is especially true now that he has emerged from misery and burial beneath history. Great poetry often arises from such dramatic conditions; gifted poets can transform great hardship and suffering into genuinely moving poems. Perhaps the greatest poets throughout history have been chosen by destiny to turn pain into profound literature. They use not just pens, but also their lives, their extraordinary fate, and their character to leave us with testimony to their times. It is because of the particular combination of Shi Zhi's fate and his creativity that his poetry has moved Chinese readers so deeply that it will be passed down from generation to generation. We might call this—following something Shi Zhi once said—"the god's art of poetry."

It is important for readers to understand Shi Zhi himself, but it is also very important for readers in English-speaking countries to pay close attention to how we evaluate his poetic legacy in China. Shi Zhi is indisputably a modern-day pioneer of Chinese poetry, a singer who has guided poets since the 1960s. He began writing five or six years earlier than Bei Dao, Mang Ke, and Duo Duo 多多, three famous Chinese poets who first wrote in the early 1970s, and he also preceded the Baiyang Lake poetry group, represented by Gen Zi 根子. Although these poets are all close to the same age, the quality of Shi Zhi's writing and the influence of his work place his poetry a full generation ahead of theirs. Even Bei Dao has talked about how he was influenced by Shi Zhi, telling a French journalist in the 1980s that the reason he wrote poetry was that he had read Shi Zhi's poetry. Duo Duo, in his 1989 article "The Buried Chinese Poets," also commented on Shi Zhi's influence on many young Beijing poets. It is clear to us now that Shi Zhi was the first poet to express different ideas and personal emotions within the idiom of the "Red fighting songs" of China's 1960s. He can thus be seen as a unique forerunner, one we might call the last poet of the Cultural Revolution and the first poet of the new era. It is also true that he was the last poet from the period of autocratic ideology and the first poet steeped in the didacticism of the modernist era.

What is particularly salient about Shi Zhi's fate is that his poetic voice is still valid. One can argue that he continues to live within history—that his writing still contributes to history. His poetry is written in out-of-date forms[1] and is imbued with old moral codes and values, yet it remains strikingly moving. Shi Zhi is a legend in contemporary China, and perhaps there are few other places in the modern world where such a legend exists. His writing is full of the melancholy beauty that has spilled over from the romantic tradition, and at the same time he is heralded as the source of the modern spirit of contemporary Chinese poetry. Taken as a whole, his work gains its power from the tragic dimensions of his unique spirit and harsh fate. He has become our witness, an embodiment of the historical rupture of the modern Chinese spirit and intellect, a bridge that connects our time to those who came before us.

Thus Shi Zhi occupies a singular place on the spiritual plane of Chinese poetry. If we say that his contemporary Huang Xiang 黄翔[2] is a manic "crazy actionist" in the mold of Don Quixote, then Shi Zhi is much more a somber and hesitant thinker like Hamlet. One is wild and the other mild, but both are descendants of Lu Xun's 鲁迅 "madman"[3] and are connected to Western romanticism. This is an important point to understand about these two writers. Because of these spiritual connections, Chinese intellectuals in the twentieth century were in line to inherit and expand the classic tradition. We can also believe that as a philosophical trend and spiritual practice, didacticism inheres and endures even when other trends appear to prevail.

While Shi Zhi's impact on Chinese poetry, poetics, and aesthetics cannot be denied, another important element of his poetry and poetics stems from his turbulent mental health history. Before 1968 his psychological condition was normal, and what would become a profoundly anxious relationship with the outside world remained largely hidden. Yet in large measure because of the historical circumstances of his rebellious youth, the conflict between the external world and the young man's inner life began to ignite his tragic imagination, which developed into the force and fount of his poetics. During his earliest period, his two representative

1. *Translator's note:* Unlike his contemporaries, Shi Zhi is known for his regular use of meter and rhyme.
2. See Huang Xiang, *A Lifetime Is a Promise to Keep: Poems of Huang Xiang,* translated and with an introduction by Michelle Yeh (Berkeley, Calif.: Institute of East Asian Studies, 2009).
3. *Translator's note:* "Lu Xun's 'madman'" is a reference to "Diary of a Madman" 狂人日记, one of Lu Xun's best known and most influential short stories. Lu Xun critiques the feudal values that still held sway over China at the beginning of the twentieth century by comparing them to cannibalism.

poems "Ocean Trilogy" and "Fish Trilogy" illuminated the basic themes of his life: his willingness to cast himself in the roles of tragic figures, and his ability to build dramatic tension between contrastive themes. Shi Zhi purposefully constructs tragically beautiful poems around failures and imagined victims. This is the most important element in making his poetry so moving. His work consistently alternates between binary oppositions such as present/future, light/dark, failure/hope, and misfortune/conviction. In his later work, these themes and his unique sense of beauty bear witness to his life. The idea of the future becomes an unfulfilled present, while the past becomes a collection of failed hopes. His poetry becomes a form of evidence, full of singular personality and thus great tragic power.

The second thematic foundation of Shi Zhi's poetics is a lyrical mode that moves from tension/struggle/stalemate to reconciliation, undergirded by the aforementioned binary motif. In his early work, such as "Fish Trilogy," he converted negative reality into an irresistible sense of destiny so that the tension between him and reality was temporarily concealed or aestheticized into pure poetry: the fish is blocked by solid ice, an irreversible misfortune that predetermines the futility and inevitable failure of resistance. But the fish, which can be construed as a portrait of the poet's adolescence, musters its youthful vitality to make its final jump, leaping out of the water only to be frozen to death by the bitter cold. "Fish Trilogy" can be viewed as Shi Zhi's own adolescent tragedy. The slight difference between this poem and Lu Xun's "Diary of a Madman" is that Shi Zhi's hero meets a tragic end and refuses to submit or compromise even after being severely admonished. But the form of this poem is really the exception within the wider context of Shi Zhi's work. In his later poetry, the theme of conflict with fate and external historical forces is resolved through a total acceptance of the world tempered by a solid conviction that the future will bring relief from the suffering of the present. Tragic persistence and tolerant struggle are thus the most touching spiritual connotations of his poetry.

In 1968, Shi Zhi was investigated by "the departments concerned" because of the wide dissemination of his poems such as "Believe in the Future" and "This Is Beijing at 4:08," an experience that deeply affected him as a young man in his early twenties. Perhaps his personality can be analyzed by means of *Hamlet*'s characters: under great pressure, his role of feigned arrogance as a poet was unconsciously exaggerated, but he consciously enforced his sense of confusion and identification with a tragic role. Despite his calm outward appearance, he did not gain any sense of security as an intellectual youth serving enforced retraining in the countryside. He returned to his ancestral hometown in Yutai County after a year and enlisted in the army shortly after February 1971. He tried to eliminate the unrealistic pressures that were being placed on him by blending into the mainstream of life, but he was plunged back into uncontrollable melancholia when he attempted to write using only the language of mainstream ideology in such poems as "Nanjing Bridge over the Yangtze River" and "Our Generation." This shows that the conflicts between his heterodox imagination and the strong disciplinary power of external society resulted in tragedy for Shi Zhi. As a result, he sank ever more deeply into confusion and insanity.

During the thirty years from 1974 to 2004, Shi Zhi endured all kinds of hardship in his middle age. But throughout those ordeals, his poetry increased in spiritual power. The series of poems he wrote in the mental hospital include "The Final Return," "A Poet's Bitter Fate," "My Youth," and "A Blessing for My Homeland." These poems—just like those that the Tang Dynasty poet Du Fu 杜甫 wrote in his later years, or those written by the German romantic poet Friedrich Hölderlin—share the tragic implications of deep frustration. Like those poets, Shi Zhi can lay claim to a biography that reveals a genuinely authentic cultural rebel as well as the spiritual depths of one who holds up the torch of life while moving steadily forward. He also expands our understanding of psychoanalysis. In my opinion, Shi Zhi has never truly been a clinically insane patient in the sense of suffering from a genuine pathology; his poetic discourse always evinces a sober, sharp, profound, and insightful thought process, much like the witty speech spoken by Hamlet in his melancholy. If Shi Zhi does in fact suffer from severe schizophrenia, he has always managed to compose perfectly formed and ordered poetry despite it. The fact remains that his poetry includes stunning logos and a spiritual depth that far exceeds his contemporaries' work, demonstrating the complexity of his inner life and his inner spiritual balance, which have been compounded but never compromised by the complexity of his mental health issues.

THE BITTER WINDS OF SHI ZHI'S ROMANTICISM: POETIC STYLE

Shi Zhi has composed many anti-orthodox poems in an unusually orthodox style. This phenomenon should be considered in more detail before his work is read. There cannot be another Shi Zhi because the tribulations he lived through have given him a special identity, and by extension, special privileges. In a sense, he is one of a kind, the type of poet who comes along only once in a lifetime; to quote the German philosopher Karl Jaspers,[4] he is a poet who cannot be imitated. Shi Zhi is one of the great narrators of China's recent past; he tells the story of how yesterday has led up to today. In the process, he has remained loyal to the poetic forms of yesterday, just as he has never failed to remain loyal to the memory and consciousness of earlier times. Shi Zhi is the only lyric poet from the former era who continues to work in that style—a true romanticist. There are two reasons for saying so: he grew up and was shaped by a romantic era of radical idealism, and he actively inherited from former generations the psychological qualities of still-earlier romantic poets, which is to say that he composes his poetry with his own blood in a lyrical style that has reestablished the traditional lyrical forms of early modern Chinese writing.

Judged on this basis, his work moves beyond a simple imitation of earlier forms of poetry by virtue of its heterodox individuality and emotional power. The principal image he has created in his poems is one of humanity, mental conflict, kindheartedness, firm convictions, sensitive emotions, unshakable willpower, and a somewhat tragic personality. The richness of this aggregate image, combined with a personal charm that is rooted in his tragic life experiences, profoundly connects us with the deepest secrets of human nature. The failures and setbacks that he feels so deeply and reveals so perceptively in his poetry inspire strong responses in his readers. In some sense, failure can arouse a reader's deepest feelings, which is why people love to read tragedies. The fish of his "Fish Trilogy" dies on the verge of spring, demonstrating that Shi Zhi pointedly acknowledges our inner inclination toward failure and its particular meanings and feelings. In "Cold Wind" (1968) he describes the winter wind as a beggar that has sincerely given everything it has but has still been deserted. The bitter wind, which is earnest and generous in its willingness to "scatter all of my silver," has become lost itself and suffers the indignity of being despised by others. This wind later became a recurrent metaphor for Shi Zhi's own spiritual suffering: "On the outside of tightly shut windows and doors, people left me / Starving, barely conscious, I wail and groan / In the end, I understand that in the world / There are people's hearts far colder than me." No other poet in recent Chinese history

---

4. Jaspers argued that "existential communication" "cannot be simulated or imitated . . . the self has its certainty in this communication, which is something absolutely historical, not recognizable from outside." See Chris Thornhill, *Karl Jaspers: Politics and Metaphysics* (New York: Routledge, 2002), 74.

has lived through such genuinely desperate experiences, and thus only Shi Zhi could have written authentically of such "cold winds." This kind of tragic self-identification gives his poetry an unmatched sympathetic (as Aristotle might say) and purified power, like a tragedy in motion. In another poem, "Destiny" (1967), he seems to have foreseen his whole life:

> My life is a withered leaf tossed and drifting
> My future, an infertile grain of barley
> If this is my destiny
> Let me sing with abandon for the wild brambles
>
> Even as their thorns puncture my heart
> My blood is like fire, red, flaming
> Creeping toward clamorous rivers
> Though my body dies, my spirit will never be silenced!

Here suffering becomes the fulcrum of his poetic expression as well as his spiritual home, and forms the basis of what we could call the peculiar character of his fate.

However, Shi Zhi is different from the majority of romantics throughout history, in that he survived his youth and has traced his own unique, if tragic, life story. His work shows us that he was long lost in his own tragic logos and could not break free. This can be seen in the late work "The Ocean at Dawn" (1985), a revival of the theme of his maiden poem "Ocean Trilogy." As a successor to the romantic spirit, Shi Zhi likes to employ the ocean as a core poetic metaphor. The constant turbulence of the ocean's frightful billows and raging waves reflects the permanent state of the poet's innermost mind. Thus this poem can undoubtedly be regarded as Shi Zhi's portrait of his spirit and soul. The ocean, subjected to too much darkness and enduring too many powerful storms, is inflicted with wounds and scars:

> Wake, wake up, dark ocean
> You have endured the oppression of night
> And have felt the long asphyxiation of darkness
> Every anxious twitch of yours
> Is an ice-cold wave
>
> . . .

It's finally awake, the dark ocean
Naked arms, luminous muscle
On the horizon at the edge of the sky
Struggling to raise the fire-red sun . . .

Perhaps the ocean is also injured
    If not, how
    Would this red pool of blood
    Float upon its skin at dawn?

Shi Zhi's tragedy is written in his heart's blood. At times it takes the form of furious social criticism. He rarely questions society explicitly; instead, he consistently describes his inner world as a place of tragic tolerance. Yet there are times when this expression bursts forth as powerful moral and ethical questioning. His 1978 masterpiece "Mad Dog" is the best example of social commentary drawn from his own mental struggles and stands as perhaps the most vivid reflection of psychological trauma in contemporary Chinese poetry:

—To those who talk sanctimoniously about human rights
    After suffering heartless ridicule
    It's hard to see myself as human
    It's as though I have become a rabid dog
    Wandering unrestrained through the world

    But I am not yet a rabid dog
    Not yet exposed to starvation and the cold
    Anyway, I wish I had become this dog
    To learn even more about the hardship of existence
    Yet I am not as good as a rabid dog!
    It would jump these walls if forced
    But I can only endure silence
    My life holds far fewer choices

    If I could really become this dog
    I would break free from these indifferent chains
    I would not hesitate for a moment
    To leave behind so-called sacred human rights

At the end of the Cultural Revolution, many poems were written to reveal scars and express various levels of introspection, but none have come close to this one, which will forever expose the incurable wounds inflicted by the crimes of an age.

Because of his timeless lyrical power, Shi Zhi's poems will continue to circulate far and wide—not only such masterpieces as "Believe in the Future," "Love Life," and "This Is Beijing at 4:08," but all of his works. This is the reward that has been bestowed upon him by his harsh and tragic destiny. The permanent themes of hope, faith, and failure that his life embodies have overflowed the banks of what these words signify in the petit bourgeois or middle-class context, where they are perennially trapped and drained of meaning. In Shi Zhi's work, their referential roots reach deep into the authentic depths of our collective history and into the actual, from which human nature and philosophy spring. Considering the full significance of his work, we can take some comfort in knowing that righteousness may still be possible even given our history.

AT STORM'S END: RENEWAL

Having endured a near-lifetime of hardship, Shi Zhi has found his way back to family and society as his legacy has become widely known and celebrated in the public sphere. This restoration began while he was still living in the asylum, where he was visited by poets and poetry lovers from all over the world. At that time, he could meet only hastily with such visitors in the asylum's narrow, cramped hallways or in the dining hall. He also began receiving numerous awards for his poetry from civilian organizations; the largest such prize was 10,000 RMB [less than $2,000 USD at the time, but still a considerable sum for the early 1990s in China] from the magazine *Wen you* 文友 (Literary Friends), published by the poet Yi Sha 伊沙. But Shi Zhi could not spend this money freely; after all, he had to buy the same generic cigarettes and eat the same terrible food as the other patients. After he checked out of the welfare house, his life began to improve greatly. Under Zhai Hanle's care, he eventually moved into a small apartment in Haiding Shangzhuang in northern Beijing, where he peacefully settled down. This remote place is far from the city center and offers him great tranquility and silence. Not far away are an open field and a small forest where Shi Zhi walks and meditates daily. When he writes a line, he chants it to the field and trees as he slowly makes his rounds. He deeply enjoys this new life, and it shows in his serene smile.

This quiet new life has directly influenced his poetry and poetics. The recent line "I bid farewell to the dark storms of my youth" is far from the sad fury or gloomy and despairing mood of his earlier works. An ever-widening lexicon of positive words now populates his work. Words such as "sunshine," "warmth," " tea," and "stroll" appear alongside the softened melancholy of phrases like "winter sun," which have come to occupy a central position in his poetic imagery. His readers and friends all hope that after his life of hardship, he will enjoy a warm and peaceful life in his later years. Since Shi Zhi's poetry has always been so tightly bound to his fate—he once said that he is "always facing his fate"—the dramatic turn in circumstances has naturally had a strong effect on his poetry, but rather than stifling his work as might have been expected, these new circumstances have given rise to a new field of possibilities for his poetry. He truthfully narrates his own life conditions and expresses his newly found joys and peace of mind, providing confirmation of his long-held poetic convictions and his honesty. As his friend and reader, I am deeply delighted for him, and I think that readers in the United States and other English-speaking countries might also be moved by such a poet: a poet of fate who has finally glimpsed some of the rainbow that follows great winds and storms. The spiritual connectivity and direct communication at the center of Shi Zhi's work has never been broken. The simple, pure truths and mercy in his work have risen from the depths of human nature and will transcend geography and language.

Translated by Jonathan Stalling

POEMS

海洋三部曲

一 波浪与海洋

喧响的波浪
深沉的海洋
引我热烈地追求
使我殷切地向往

因为我有时惆怅
所以我喜爱大海宽阔的胸膛
因为我有时懦弱
所以我喜爱大海的无比坚强

这是因为我能力寻常
所以我渴求大海的巨大力量
这是因为我形体丑陋
所以我酷爱大海的碧蓝和明朗

我将永远为你歌唱
那喧响激昂的波浪
我将永远为你倾倒
那碧蓝深沉的海洋

二 再也掀不起波浪的海

不! 朋友, 还是远远地离开
离开这再也掀不起波浪的海
我噙着热泪劝你
去寻找灿烂的未来

远远地离开它吧
离开这再也掀不起波浪的海
它已沦落安息
像屋檐下过夜的乞丐

失去了青春的热情
失去了言语的坦白
然而更可怕的——
是失去了正直的胸怀

朋友, 你为什么流泪了
要哭就索性哭个痛快
不是哭它那逝去的青春
而是哭那颗曾经战斗的灵魂

 **OCEAN TRILOGY**

1. Waves and Ocean

Clamorous waves
And a deep ocean
Fervently attract me
And eagerly draw me forward

When I am depressed
I find solace in its broad chest
When I am weak
I need its unwavering resolution

It is because I am so ordinary
That I yearn for the ocean's great power
It is because I appear so homely
That I love its deep, luminous blue

I will always sing of you
Of your loud, impassioned waves
I will always bow before you
Before this deep ocean blue

2. The Ocean without Waves

No! Friend, get as far away as you can
Leave this ocean that can no longer lift its waves
With scalding tears, I beg you
Go search for your own promising future

Get as far away as you can
Leave this ocean without waves
It has fallen fast asleep
Like someone homeless dozing under an eave at night

It has lost its youthful vigor
Even its honest voice
Worse still
It has lost its righteous spirit

My friend, why are you crying
Let it out if you need to
Just don't cry over its lost youth
Cry instead for its ever-fighting spirit

远远地离开这沉默的海吧
但千万千万不要忘记
它也曾一度波涛澎湃
汹涌不息地奔向未来

如今，它可怕地沉默了
多少感情在它心中藏埋
它仍然积蓄着力量
它还在焦急地等待……

不！朋友，还是远远地离开
远远地离开……留下我自己
守着这再也掀不起波浪的海
蹒跚地踱步，徘徊

三 给朋友们

——少用眼泪叙说悲欢
多写诗歌赞美勇敢

1
"开船嘞——"
激动的风热情地召唤
一种令人振奋的喜悦
把声音传得很远很远

不是到一起重温旧梦
而是再一次并肩作战
我年轻的战友啊
快快扬帆解缆

就这条可怜的小船
也配作红卫兵远航的兵舰
算了吧！酒桌旁的醉汉
生活的道路从来就不平坦

"生活的欢乐就是挥霍金钱
勇气将能换来丰富的酒宴"
可耻
一副拜金者贪婪的嘴脸

也有人在和爱神一起消磨时间
草掩的荒径走过年轻的侣伴
他们不再渴望暴风雨的欢乐
而只沉湎于小家庭的温暖

Please get as far away from this silent ocean as you can
Yet never, ever forget
How its waves once surged forward
Rushing headlong into the future

Today it remains unbearably silent
How many feelings lie buried within
It is still saving its power
Anxiously waiting for its time . . .

No! Friend, get as far away as you can
Leave me here alone . . .
So that I can stay with this waveless sea
Staggering, hesitating

3. For Friends

—Fewer tears should be used to express grief and joy
Instead, more poems should be used to praise bravery

1
"Set Sail—"
Passionate winds call out to me
An excited joy takes hold
And carries this voice far, so far away

We are not reunited by our old dreams
But fight shoulder-to-shoulder once more
Young comrades-in-arms
Quickly, hoist the sails and unfasten the cables

This wretched little boat
Cannot be used as the Red Guard's warship
Forget it! A drunk leaning against the table
Life's road is never a smooth one

"Life's pleasures are but money squandered
Courage can always be exchanged for a feast"
Shameless
The greed-contorted face of a money worshipper

There are those who spend their days with the God of Love
Young lovers walking down grass-covered paths
No longer yearn for the joy of the storm
But lose themselves in the warmth of their little families

"开船嘞——"
失望的风呜咽地呼唤
止不住的热泪扑向沙滩
把几行远行者的脚印吻舔

2
我突然心酸地觉察到
握住桨的手臂是那样弱小
远航者的行装，衣着
又是那样朴素，单薄

一套毛泽东选集
贴身放在火热的胸前
一枚毛主席像章
夕阳辉映下金色灿烂

一身洗白的军衣
曾跟从父母经受烽火的考验
一条军用的皮带
也伴随孩子历尽风浪的惊险……

高举起向岸边挥动的哟
是再见的手臂
簌簌淋落胸前的哟
是别离的泪雨

一位霜发老人匆匆赶来送行
深陷的眼眶里热泪晶莹
"孩子啊，要把握住前进的方向
必须双眼不离北斗星"

深情的嘱托絮絮的叮咛
乘驾海风随帆船飘零
待海风再把它们送回岸上
已化为令人心碎的桨声

3
这夜，深远的夜空星光黯淡
狂风在命运的海洋里燃起狼烟
落了帆的小船是一匹狂颠的战马
扬起的脖颈上带着鲜血和勇敢

"Set Sail—"
The dejected wind calls out, sobbing
Warm tears fall upon the sand
And kiss the footprints of those who have left for distant lands

2

Suddenly I realize from the depths of my grief
That the arms behind the oars are so puny
And the sailor's clothes and bags
Are so flimsy and cheap

Mao Tse-tung's collected works
Are tightly clasped to his warm chest
A Chairman Mao badge
Glows golden under the setting sun

A washed-out army uniform
Has endured the flames of war with his parents
And the army belt
Now follows the children to experience the storm

Held high, waving toward the shore
Are farewell's arms
Sss sss, thickly raining down the chest
Are departure's tears

A graying old man hurries to send him off
Sunken eyes glimmering with tears
"My child, never stop moving forward
Keep your eyes on the Big Dipper"

With a soft, deeply trusting warning
He drifts away with the winds, sailing
As the winds carry them back to shore
They are little more than the aching sounds of oars

3

Tonight the infinite sky is only dimly lit by stars
Gales ignite beacons across the ocean of fate
Its sail lowered, the boat is an unbridled warhorse
Courageously lifting its bloody mane

它突然跌进浪谷
沉埋在无底的深渊
在哪儿，在哪儿啊
我所期望的帆船……

呜咽的风啊掀起滔天的浪
精神的船啊划动着意志的桨
这儿已不是递送微笑的沙龙
我们正踏进流着鲜血的战场

像秋风卷走一张枯叶
命运的海洋啊
你将把这条船带向何方
地狱呢？还是天堂

"快把船靠向我们，靠向左边
这里是鱼儿群居的海湾"
声音从左边极远的方向传来
原来是一只在命运的海洋里谋利的渔船

"让暴风雨来得更猛烈些吧"
这是海洋深处被压抑的呼唤
"让胆怯的死亡吧
活着的将更加勇敢"

看哪！我们的小船
它已昂首于浪巅
瞧她那高傲自大的神气
多像一只得意洋洋的海燕

．．．．．．．．．．．．．．．．．．
．．．．．．．．．．．．．．．．．

朋友，请不要用目光问我
这样结束是不是有些突然
只待暴风雨式的生活过去
再给我们留下热情真挚的语言

Suddenly falling into a valley of waves
It is buried in limitless depths
Where, where has it gone
The sailboat I have hoped for

Wailing winds push waves into the sky
Spirit craft, propelled by oars of will
This is no longer a smiling solon
But a blood-covered battlefield

Like an autumn wind sweeping away a fallen leaf
Oceanic fate
Where are you leading this boat?
To hell? Or heaven?

"Pull the boat closer, keep left
This is a bay of schooling fish"
A sound arrives from far off on the left
From a fishing boat trolling the sea of fate for profit

"Let the storm break in all its fury!"*
A suppressed yell from deep beneath the ocean echoes
"Let the cowards die
The living will be all the more courageous"**

Look, our small boat
It's riding the crest of a wave
You can see her arrogant manner
Like a proud petrel

. . .
. . .

My friend, please don't ask me with your eyes
Whether an end like this is too abrupt
Just wait for the torrent of life to pass
Then leave us your passionate and sincere words

First draft, February 1965/final version, February 1, 1968

---

* This is a line from the Russian poet Maxim Gorky's "Song of the Stormy Petrel," a poem famous in Mao's China.
** This is also a line from "Song of the Stormy Petrel."

书简 （一）

这首诗为一幅画像而作，画像是十二月党人之妻在丈夫临服苦役前送别时送给她爱人的。

忧郁之神征服了你
我亲爱的妻——
他同样折磨着我
使我不时痛苦地忆起你

但我必须将一切忧郁摒弃
因为自由之神需要我活下去
要不，谁来坚守我们的要塞
谁去夺取敌人的阵地

每当我想到活下去
我就更加思念你
每当我想到活下去
我就联想到坦白忠诚的友谊

难道在人生艰难的旅途里
上帝不再赐予我们轻松的步履
难道我们昨日的无限情意
仅仅是为了今天痛苦的别离

我们应当永远牢记一条真理
无论在欢乐还是辛酸的日子里
我们的心啊，要永远向前憧憬
这样，才不会丧失生活的勇气

…………

这张画像画得真好
不是指你美丽的容颜
而是指你圣洁的心地

为了感谢你
对我爱情的忠贞不渝
愿北去的春风代替我
热烈地吻你，我亲爱的妻

THE LETTER, PART ONE

*This poem was inspired by a portrait of a woman that was given to her husband,
a Decembrist, before he was sent to a labor camp.**

The god of melancholia has overtaken you
My dear wife—
He tortures me as well and
Calls you back into memory time and again

Yet I cannot abandon myself to grief
Because the god of liberty needs me alive
Who else will defend our garrison
Who else will seize the enemy's position?

Whenever I think of living on
I miss you all the more
Whenever I think of living on
I am reminded of your pure devotion

Is it possible that in life's hard travels
God no longer lightens our loads?
Is it possible that yesterday's endless love
Will only sharpen today's bitter farewells?

We must always plant truth firmly in our minds
In times of joy and misery
Our hearts must always look forward
So we don't lose our courage forever

. . .

Your portrait is wonderfully drawn
Not because you look so beautiful
But because it reveals your divine heart

To thank you
For your steadfast love
I pray to the northern spring winds
To kiss you full, my dear wife

1965

---

* The Decembrist revolt/uprising took place in imperial Russia on December 14,
1825. Russian army officers led about 3,000 soldiers in a protest against Nicholas I's
ascension to the throne. The revolt was subsequently crushed, and its supporters
were killed and imprisoned.

书简（二）

真实地告诉我
苦役中的爱人
是谁向你透露出
我心中难言的痛苦

是那伤心中呆滞的目光
还是忧郁中憔悴的面容
是过度的思念中消瘦的双颊
还是痛苦的嘴唇上留下的齿痕

淡漠无际的哀愁啊
果真是培育爱情的园丁
维纳斯啊，不再是会心的微笑
而化做一双失神的眼睛

真实地告诉我，苦役中的爱人
在仆仆万里的风尘中
爱情可增加了你征途的沉重
泪水可曾潮湿过你的眼睛

真实地告诉我，苦役中的爱人
高举的皮鞭下可还有醉心的恬静
肮脏的辱骂里可也有深切的同情
想到这些，我的心就猛烈地撞击着胸

彼得格勒还在雪毯下冬眠
西伯利亚却早已是万物苏醒
彼得格勒还是茫茫无边的黑夜
西伯利亚却早已是朝阳喷薄的黎明

真实地告诉我，苦役中的爱人
西伯利亚可也有纷乱的葛藤
葛藤上可也密织过希望的绿叶
枯枝上的露水可也像眼泪一样晶莹

告诉我呵，还要告诉我
我们要到何时才能相逢
是在明年枝挂绿叶
还是就在今年，等风雪飘零……

 ## THE LETTER, PART TWO

Tell me the truth
My imprisoned love
Who revealed to you
The unspeakable grief I endure?

Is it the darkened sight of misery
Or the thinned face of melancholy
Is it the cheeks atrophied by forever waiting
Or the teeth marks left on painful lips

Faint and endless grief
Is really love's gardener
Venus, no longer a knowing smile,
Is but a pair of glazed eyes

Tell me the truth, my imprisoned love
Across a thousand miles of exhausting wind and dirt
Has love embittered you with an even greater burden
Or have tears moistened your eyes?

Tell me the truth, my imprisoned love
Under the leather whip can you still lose yourself in peace?
Amid their crude insults is there any sympathy?
Thinking of these, my heart pounds violently against my chest

St. Petersburg is still hibernating under a quilt of snow
As Siberia has long since begun to revive
While St. Petersburg still waits under an endless night
Siberia has already begun to rush toward dawn

Tell me the truth, my imprisoned love
Does Siberia have entangled vines nearby?
Are there green leaves of hope densely woven into them?
Is the dew forming on deadwood glittering like tears?

Tell me, do tell me one more time
When will we meet again?
Will it be next year as green leaves hang from branches
Or this year, snow drifting in the wind?

1967

命 运

好的声望是永远找不开的钞票，
坏的名声是永远挣不脱的枷锁，
如果事实真是这样的话，
我愿在单调的海洋上终生 摸索 漂泊。

哪儿找得到结实的舢板，
我只有在街头四处流落，
只希望敲到朋友的门前，
能得到一点菲薄的施舍。

我的一生是辗转飘零的枯叶，
我的未来是抽不出锋芒的青稞；
如果命运真是这样的话，
我愿为野生的荆棘高歌。

哪怕荆棘刺破我的心，
火一样的血浆火一样地燃烧着，
挣扎着爬进喧闹的江河，
人死了，精神永不沉默！

 **DESTINY**

A good reputation is a banknote that can never be broken
A bad reputation is a chain from which one cannot break free
If this is the nature of the real world
Let me drift forever on the monotony of the sea

Where can I find a reliable raft?
Destitute, I can only wander empty city streets
Looking for a friendly door to knock on
To bum at least a little change

My life is a withered leaf tossed and drifting
My future, an infertile grain of barley
If this is my destiny
Let me sing with abandon for the wild brambles

Even as their thorns puncture my heart
My blood is like fire, red, flaming
Creeping toward clamorous rivers
Though my body dies, my spirit will never be silenced!

1967

鱼儿三部曲

一

冷漠的冰层下鱼儿顺水而去，
听不到一声鱼儿痛苦的叹息，
既然得不到一点温暖的阳光，
又怎能迎送生命中绚烂的朝夕？！

现实中没有波浪，
可怎么浴血搏击？
前程呵，远不可测，
又怎能把希望托寄？

鱼儿精神*唯一的安慰，
便是沉湎于甜蜜的回忆。
让那痛苦和欢欣的眼泪，
再次将淡淡的往事托起。

既不是春潮中追逐的花萼，
也不是骄阳下恬静的安息；
既不是初春的寒风料峭，
也不是仲夏的绿水涟漪。

而是当大自然缠上白色的绷带，
流着鲜血的伤口刚刚合愈。
地面已不再有徘徊不定的枯叶，
天上也不再挂深情缠绵的寒雨。

它是怎样猛烈地跳跃呵，
为了不失去自由的呼吸；
它是怎样疯狂地反扑呵，
为了不失去鱼儿的利益。

虽然每次反扑总是失败，
虽然每次弹跃总是碰壁，
然而勇敢的鱼儿并不死心，
还在积蓄力量作最后的努力。

终于寻到了薄弱环节，
好呵，弓起腰身弹上去，
低垂的尾首腾空跃展，
那么灵活又那么有力！

---

* The characters 精神 have been added.

 **FISH TRILOGY**

I

Beneath layers of indifferent ice, a fish flows with the current
Its bitter sighs cannot be heard
Since it cannot find any warm sunlight
Why would it greet and send off the glorious day?

If there are no waves in reality
Why does it bathe in the blood of struggle?
If its future is distant beyond measure
How can it take refuge in hope?

Fish can only find spiritual solace
In sweet memory
Let its bittersweet tears
Again hold up the pale stories of the past

It is not the time for chasing blooms in spring winds
Or resting peacefully beneath the summer sun
Nor is it the time for feeling the chill of early spring winds
Or seeing the rippling green water of midsummer

But it's when nature is covered in white bandages
And the bleeding wounds have just healed
There are no more withered leaves lingering on the ground
Or cold rain endlessly falling from the sky

How fiercely it leaps from the water
To not lose the freedom of breath
How wildly it strikes back
To not lose what advantages it still may possess

Though every leap ends in failure
Every jump falls short
Yet the steely fish still has the nerve
To hold back for the final push

At last finding a thin patch of ice
Yes, it bends back like a bow and springs
With head down and tail extended, it soars into the air
So nimble, so strong

一束淡淡的阳光投到水里，
轻轻抚摸着鱼儿带血双鳍；
"孩子呵，这是今年最后的一面，
下次相会怕要到明年的春季。"

鱼儿迎着阳光愉快欢跃着，
不时露出水面自由地呼吸。
鲜红的血液溶进缓缓的流水，
顿时舞作疆场上飘动的红旗。

突然，一阵剧烈的疼痛，
使鱼儿昏迷，沉向水底。
我的鱼儿啊，你还年轻，
怎能就这样结束一生？！

不要再沉了，不要再沉了，
我的心呵，在低声地喃语。
……终于鱼儿苏醒过来了，
又拼命向着阳光游去。

当它再一次把头露出水面，
这时鱼儿已经竭尽全力。
冰冷的嘴唇还在无声地翕动，
波动的水声已化作高傲的口气：

"永不畏惧冷酷的的风雪，
绝不俯仰寒冬的鼻息。"
说罢，返身扎向水底，
头也不回地向前游去……

冷漠的冰层下鱼儿顺水漂去，
听不到一声鱼儿痛苦的叹息。
既然得不到一点温暖的阳光，
又何必迎送生命中绚烂的朝夕？！

二

趁着夜色，凿开冰洞，
渔夫匆忙地设下了网绳。
堆放在岸边的食品和烟丝，
朦胧中等待着蓝色的黎明。

Faint sunlight ripples through the water
Gently stroking its bleeding fins
My child, I'm afraid this may be our last encounter
Until we meet next spring

Facing the sun, it joyously jumps again
Able to breathe above the water now and then
Its wisps of crimson blood disperse into the stream
Waving like red flags upon the battlefield

Suddenly, with a spasm of sharp pain,
It sinks unconscious into the depths
Oh my fish, you are still young
How can this be your end?!

Stop sinking, stop sinking
My heart babbles in its hushed voice
Finally snapping awake
Desperate, it flashes toward the sunlight

When it emerges from the water again
It has given its all
Cold lips opening and closing without a sound
From the undulating water rises a noble voice

"Never fear the callous wind and snow
Never surrender to the bitter winter's breath"
Voice fading, it plunges back into the water
Without looking back, it swims onward

Beneath layers of indifferent ice, a fish slides with the current
Its suffering moans cannot be heard
Since it cannot find any warm sunlight
Why should it meet and send off the glorious day?

II

Cutting a hole in the ice beneath the cover of night
A fisherman quickly sets his nets
Provisions of food and tobacco stacked on the shore
Enveloped in clouds, he waits for the blue-gray dawn

为什么悬垂的星斗象眼泪一样晶莹？
难道黑暗之中也有真实的友情？
但为什么还没等到鱼儿得到暗示，
黎明的手指就摘落了满天慌乱的寒星？

一束耀眼的灿烂阳光，
晃得鱼儿睁不开眼睛，
暖化了冰层冻结的夜梦
慈爱地将沉睡的鱼儿唤醒：

"我的孩子呵，可还认识我？
可还叫得出我的姓名？
可还在寻找我命运的神谕？
可仍然追求自由与光明？"

鱼儿听到阳光的询问，
睁开了迷惘失神的眼睛，
试着摇动麻木的尾翼，
双鳍不时拍拂着前胸：

"自由的阳光，真实地告诉我，
这可是希望的春天来临？
岸边可放下难吃的鱼饵？
天空可已有归雁的行踪？"

沉默呵，沉默，可怕的沉默，
得不到一丝一毫的回声。
鱼儿的心突然颤抖了，
它听到树枝在嘶喊着苦痛。

警觉催促它立即前行，
但鱼儿痴恋这一线光明，
它还想借助这缕阳光，
看清楚自己渺茫的前程……

当鱼儿完全失去了希望，
才看清了身边狰狞的网绳。
"春天在哪儿呵，"它含着眼泪
重又开始了冰层下的旅程。

象渔夫咀嚼食品那样，
阳光撕破了贪婪的网绳。
在烟丝腾起的云雾之中，
渔夫做着丰收的美梦。

Why do the suspended stars glitter like translucent tears?
Can there be true friendship in the dark?
Why has the fish not yet discovered
That the fingers of dawn have already plucked the cold, rattling stars?

A brilliant ray of sunlight flashes
And the fish can barely open its eyes
It thaws dreams frozen in the ice
And gently wakes the fish from its deep sleep

"Oh my child, do you still remember me?
Can you call out my name?
Are you still searching for the destiny I have written for you?
Are you still searching for freedom and the light?"

Hearing the sun's questions
The fish opens its baffled eyes
It attempts to shake its numb tail
A pair of fins gently patting its breast

"Sunshine of freedom, please tell me the truth
Is this the spring of hope?
Is there inedible bait lying off the shore?
Are there any traces of returning geese in the sky?"

Silence, silence, awful silence
It can't throw even the faintest echo
The fish's heart quivers in a jolt
It hears branches screaming in pain

Vigilance urges the fish directly forward
Infatuated with the sun's glow
It wants to cast the sun's radiance down across
The vague road of its future . . .

Only when all hope is lost
Does the fish see the ferocious nets closing in
"Where is spring?" tears pooling in its eyes
Again it begins its journey beneath the ice

Like the fisherman devouring his food
The sun tears through his insatiable nets
In the rising cloud of his tobacco
The fisherman dreams of a bountiful harvest

三

苏醒的春天终于盼来了，
阳光的利剑显示了威力，
无情地割裂冰封的河面，
冰块在河床里挣扎撞击。

冰层下睡了一年多的水蟒，
刚露头又赶紧缩回河底，
荣称为前线歌手的青蛙，
也吓得匆忙向四方逃匿。

我的鱼儿，我的鱼儿呵，
你在哪里，你在哪里？
你盼了一冬，就是死了，
也该浮上来你的尸体！

真的，鱼儿真的死了，
眼睛象是冷漠的月亮，
刚才微微翕动的鳃片，
现在象平静下去的波浪。

是因为它还年轻，性格又倔强，
它对于自由与阳光的热切盼望，
使得它不顾一切跃出了水面，
但却落在了终将消融的冰块上。

鱼儿临死前在冰块上拼命地挣扎着
太阳急忙在云层后收起了光芒——
是她不忍心看到她的孩子，
年轻的鱼儿竟是如此下场。

鱼儿却充满献身的欲望：
"太阳，我是你的儿子，
快快抽出你的利剑啊，
我愿和冰块一同消亡！"

真的，鱼儿真的死了，
眼睛象是冷漠的月亮，
刚才微微翕动的鳃片，
现在象平静下去的波浪。

III

So long desired, spring's revival finally arrives
The sun's long, sharp blade reveals its power
And callously severs the icebound river
As sheets of struggling ice crash together

Beneath layers of ice, a python has slept the year through
Barely emerging, it swiftly withdraws to the river bottom
The frogs, wearing the banners of battlefield singers,
Are frightened and scurry in all directions to hide

My fish, my fish
Where are you, where have you gone?
Have you yearned for winter, and if you did die
Your body should float up to the surface!

It's true, the fish really did die
Its dull eyes are as pale as the moon
Just now, its gills moved so faintly
Falling back like quiet waves

It was still so young, so headstrong
Because it so fervently sought the sun and its freedom
It leapt from the water without fear of the consequences
Only to fall upon the ice, which will melt in time

At the point of death, the fish struggled upon the ice
The sun quickly hid its light behind the clouds
Unwilling to watch her child
Such a young fish to share this fate

But the fish was ready to give his life
"Sun, I am your child
Please pull out your sharp sword
Let me dissolve together with the ice"

It's true, the fish really did die
Its dull eyes are as pale as the indifferent moon
Just now, its gills moved so faintly
Falling back like quiet waves

一张又一张新春的绿叶，
无风自落，纷纷扬扬，
和着泪滴一样的细雨，
把鱼儿的尸体悄悄埋葬。

是一堆锋芒毕露的鱼骨，
还是堆丰富的精神矿藏，
我的灵魂那绿色坟墓，
可会引人深思和遐想……

当这冰块已消亡，
河水也不再动荡。
草丛里蹦来青蛙，
浮藻中游出水蟒。

水蟒吃饱了，静静听着，
青蛙动人的慰问演唱。
水蟒同情地流出了眼泪，
当青蛙唱到鱼儿的死亡。

One newborn leaf after another
Falls without wind, scattering through the air
With a faint tear-like rain
To cover the dead fish in silence

Is it a heap of sharp white bones
Or a rich storehouse of spirit?
My soul, its green tomb,
Will it provoke deep, wandering thoughts?

When the ice has dissolved
And the river relaxes its waves
Frogs leap from the grass
Pythons swim out from the algae

After a full meal, the pythons listen quietly
To the frogs' elegiac songs
And weep piteous tears
When the frogs sing of the fish's death

1967–1968

烟

燃起的香烟中飘出过未来的幻梦，
蓝色的云雾是挣扎过希望的黎明。
而如今这烟缕却成了我心中的愁绪，
汇成了低沉的含雨未落的云层。

我推开明亮的玻璃窗，
迎进郊外田野的清风。
多想留住飘散的烟缕——
那是你向我告别的身影。

 **SMOKE**

From a lit cigarette, a dream of the future rises
The blue cloud is the dawn of hope once struggled for
But now it becomes a fog of depression in my heart
Condensed into a deep cloud of unfalling rain

I push open the bright window
To greet the refreshing rural breeze
How I long to hold on to the fading smoke
That is your shadow bidding me farewell

Summer 1968

酒

火红的酒浆仿佛是热血酿成，
欢乐的酒杯里盛满疯狂的热情。
如今，酒杯在我手中颤栗，
波动中仍有你一双美丽的眼睛。

我已在欢乐之中沉醉，
但是为了心灵的安宁，
我还要干了这一杯，
喝尽你那一片痴情。

WINE

As if brewed from blood, a fire-red wine
Overflows a euphoric glass with fervor
The glass trembles in my hand
As your beautiful eyes appear upon the sloshing wine

I am drunk with joy
But for the peace of my soul
I will finish this off
Drinking down all of your passion

Summer 1968

我这样说

当那秋风吹散黄金的落叶
像是令人心碎的告别的幽咽
宁静的雨水掺和着苦涩的眼泪
斟满了我们手中颤栗的酒杯

当在秋天伤心的黎明
甜蜜的瓜果离开了枝头
果枝和藤蔓含着秋露
永别了她那心爱的朋友

一个声音在缠绵地叙说
"朋友记着我，永远记着我"
是的，我这样说

随着时光麻木地流逝
你将失去美好的回忆
悄悄飘落的白玉兰的花瓣
怜爱地铺满了丰收后的大地

也许这时真的到了
白花为我开放的时候
我把脚印留给死亡
仍然向着未来奔走

一个声音在冰冷地叙说
"朋友忘掉我，永远忘掉我"
是的，我这样说

 **THIS IS WHAT I SAY**

When autumn winds scatter golden leaves
Heartbroken, I feel the murmuring farewell of mourning
A gentle rain mixing with bitter tears
Fills the trembling wineglasses in our hands

In autumn a broken-hearted day breaks
A honied fruit falls from its stem
Fruit-bearing branches and vines full of dew
Her beloved friends are forever left behind

A poignant voice speaks out:
"Friends, remember me, always remember me"
Yes, this is what I say

As time passes numbly
You will lose your finer memories
Like quietly falling orchid petals
Quilting Mother Earth with their bounty

Perhaps it is the right time
When white flowers open for me
I leave footprints behind for death
Still running on toward the future

A cold voice speaks out
"Friends, forget me, forget me forever"
Yes, this is what I say

Autumn 1968

这是四点零八分的北京

这是四点零八分的北京，
一片手的海洋翻动；
这是四点零八分的北京，
一声雄伟的汽笛长鸣。

北京车站高大的建筑，
突然一阵剧烈的抖动。
我双眼吃惊地望着窗外，
不知发生了什么事情。

我的心骤然一阵疼痛，一定是
妈妈缀扣子的针线穿透了心胸。
这时，我的心变成了一只风筝，
风筝的线绳就在妈妈手中。

线绳绷得太紧了，就要扯断了，
我不得不把头探出车厢的窗棂。
直到这时，直到这时候，
我才明白发生了什么事情。

——一阵阵告别的声浪，
　　就要卷走车站；
　　北京在我的脚下，
　　已经缓缓地移动。

我再次向北京挥动手臂，
想一把抓住他的衣领，
然后对她大声地叫喊：
永远记着我，妈妈啊，北京！

终于抓住了什么东西，
管他是谁的手，不能松，
因为这是我的北京，
这是我的最后的北京。

☀ THIS IS BEIJING AT 4:08

This is Beijing at 4:08
An ocean of waving hands
This is Beijing at 4:08
A grand train whistle trailing off

Beijing station's towering edifice
Convulses without warning
Shaken, I look out the windows
Not knowing what's going on

My heart shudders in pain; it must be
My mother's sewing needle runs me through
At this moment my heart transforms into a kite
Tethered to her hands

So tight it may snap
I have to stick my head out the train window
Up till now, till this very moment,
I begin to understand what has happened

—A fit of parting shouts
    Is about to sweep away the train station
    Beijing still underfoot
    Slowly begins to drift away

Once more I wave to Beijing
And I want to grab her by the collar
And shout to her
Remember me, Mother Beijing!

I've grasped something at last
No matter whose hand it is—I'll never let go
For this is my Beijing
This is my last Beijing

December 20, 1968

冬夜月台送别

那声声高喊呼叫的汽笛啊
为什么今天叫得这样凄惨
是按到年轻人不均匀的脉搏
还是看到了车窗上噙着泪的双眼

那日日奔波不停的列车啊
如今却知情地迟迟不前
走你的路吧，命运的漂泊者
流浪汉尝不到爱情的甘甜

如水的月光洗着贫寒的树尖
凛冽的寒风掀扬起年轻人的发卷
俯身拾不到一片寄情的枯叶
愿诗句记下这月台深冬的夜晚

FAREWELL FROM THE PLATFORM ON A WINTER'S NIGHT

The steam whistle wails again and again
Why is today so miserable?
Is it because it touches the uneven pulse of the young
Or sees the welled-up eyes through the window?

The train, rushing on day after day,
Seems to understand their sorrow and refuses to move forward
Walk on, fate's drifter
A vagrant could never taste the sweetness of love

Watery moonlight washes the cold tops of trees
Bitter winds lift the young man's curls
Reaching down, I cannot find even a withered leaf to express my
    emotion
Let my poem be a record of this platform on a winter's night

Winter 1968

还是干脆忘掉她吧

还是干脆忘掉她吧，
乞丐寻不到人世的温存，
我清楚地看到未来，
漂泊才是命运的女神。

眼泪可是最贴心的爱人，
就像夜露亲吻着花唇，
苦涩里流露着浸心的甘美，
甘美中寻不到一屑俗尘。

幻想可是最迷人的爱人，
就像月光织绣的长裙，
想起来是嫦娥的愁绪，
看到的是素白的单纯。

缪斯可是最漂亮的爱人，
就象展翅飞起的鸽群，
迅速 地消失在我的蓝天里，
只留下鸽铃那袅袅的余音。

眼泪幻想啊终将竭尽，
缪斯也将眠于荒坟。
是等爱人抛弃我呢？
还是我先抛弃爱人？

还是干脆忘掉她吧，
乞丐寻不到人世的温存。
我清楚地看到未来，
漂泊才是命运的女神。

IT WOULD BE BEST TO SIMPLY FORGET HER

It would be best to simply forget her
A beggar can find little tenderness in this world
I can see the future clearly
The goddess of destiny is a vagabond

Yet tears may be the most intimate lover
Like night dew kissing flowered lips
Only in suffering is sweetness revealed
Which doesn't contain even the slightest earthly dust

Fantasy may be the most enchanting lover
Like a gown woven from moonlight
Which might be Chang E's grief
When seen, it is simply pure whiteness

Muse may be the most beautiful lover
Like the spreading wings of pigeons taking flight
Vanishing swiftly into my blue sky
And leaving only traces of pigeon whistles on the wind

Yet tears and fantasies will finally dry up
One's muse will make its bed in a desolate grave
Will I wait for my lover to abandon me?
Or will I be the one to abandon her first?

So just forget her
Beggars can find little tenderness in this world
I can see the future clearly
The goddess of destiny is a vagabond

Late 1968

你们相爱

你们相爱不是在春天里
幸运啊，年轻忠实的伴侣
既然没有妩媚的花容
也就不会有痛苦的别离

你们相爱不是在夏天
不像流水中相逢的浮莲
萍叶的前程总是分手啊
生活的激流一向急湍

你们相爱不是在秋天
不是在果实累累的田园
也不像秋风摘落的枯叶
在和秋雨深情地缠绵

你们相爱是在冷酷的冬天
当命运的河流上凝浮着厚厚的冰寒
然而，谁也没有能力来遏止啊
冰层下感情的暖流奔腾向前

 ## YOU ARE IN LOVE

You are not in love in the spring
Thankfully you are young and loyal companions
Since you don't have graceful faces like flowers
You will not have a painful parting

You are not in love in the summer
Unlike duckweed touching upon a flowing stream
For they will part ways forever
The rushing currents of life always sweep them onward

You are not in love in the autumn
Not in orchards heavy with fruit
Or like withered leaves plucked by winds
Enmeshed so deeply in autumn rain

You are in love through the frigid winter
When thick sheets of ice float upon the frozen river of fate
But no one has the power to hold back
The warm currents of emotion rushing beneath its ice

1968

相信未来

当蜘蛛网无情地查封了我的炉台
当灰烬的余烟叹息着贫困的悲哀
我依然固执地铺平失望的灰烬
用美丽的雪花写下: 相信未来

当我的紫葡萄化为深秋的泪*水
当我的鲜花依偎在别人的情怀
我依然固执地用凝露**的枯藤
在凄凉的大地上写下: 相信未来

我要用手指, 那涌向天边的排浪
我要用手掌, 那托起***太阳的大海
摇曳着曙光那枝温暖漂亮的笔杆
用孩子的笔体写下: 相信未来

我之所以坚定地相信未来
是我相信未来人们的眼睛—
她有拨开历史风尘的睫毛
她有看透岁月篇章的瞳孔

不管人们对于我们腐烂的皮肉
那些迷途的惆怅, 失败的苦痛
是寄予感动的热泪, 深切的同情
还是轻蔑的微笑, 辛辣的嘲讽

我坚信人们对于我们的脊骨
那无数次的探索, 迷途, 失败和成功
一定会给予热情, 客观, 公正的评定
是的, 我焦急地等待着他们的评定

朋友, 坚定地相信未来吧
相信不屈不挠的努力
相信战胜死亡的年轻
相信未来, 热爱生命

---

* The popular version of this poem, memorized by the Red Guard generation, contained the character for "dew" 露 here instead of "tears" 泪.

** The character 霜 has been changed to 露.

*** The character 住 has been changed to 起. The commas were added as well.

 **BELIEVE IN THE FUTURE**

As spider webs mercilessly seal off my stovetop
As smoldering cinders sigh over the sorrows of poverty
I still stubbornly spread out the hopeless cinders
And write with finely powdered snow: believe in the future

As my purple grapes dissolve into late-autumn tears
As my flower leans upon another's breast
I still stubbornly reach for a frozen, withered vine
And write upon the desolate ground: believe in the future

I want to surge my fingers like waves past the horizon
I want to hold up the sun with my palms above the ocean
With dawn's first flickering rays on my warm, fine pen
I write in a child's handwriting: believe in the future

I firmly believe in the future because
I have faith in the future of humanity's eyes—
Her eyelashes will push aside the harrowing history
Her pupils will pierce through the chapters of time

Regardless of how other people treat our rotting flesh
The grief of losing one's way and the pain of failure
With either their moving tears, their deep sympathy
Or their contemptuous sneers and caustic scorn

I firmly believe in the backbone of our humanity
It will give us warm, objective, and fair judgment
Of the numerous searches, strayings, failures, and successes
Yes, I anxiously await their pronouncement

Friend, believe unfailingly in the future
Believe in the never-bending struggle
Believe in death-conquering youth
Believe in the future, and love life

1968

难道爱神是……

难道爱神是焦渴的唇
只顾痛饮殷红的血，晶莹的泪
而忘却了在血泊中
还有两颗跳动的心

难道爱神是纤细的手
只醉心于拨弄心弦的琴
而忘却了在颤抖中
还有两颗痛苦的心

难道爱神是无踪影的风
只顾追逐天堂上轻浮的云
而忘却了在地狱中
还有两颗沉重的心

难道爱神是心舟的桨
无意间摇碎了月儿在湖心的印
而忘却了在波动中
还有两颗破碎的心

ISN'T THE GOD OF LOVE NOT MORE THAN ...

Is the God of Love not more than thirsty lips
Selfishly drinking down dark red blood and crystalline tears
Yet forgetting that within this crimson pool
There are still two beating hearts

Is the God of Love not more than slender hands
Playing with infatuation upon heartstrings
Yet forgetting that in their quivering
There are still two suffering hearts

Is the God of Love not more than traceless wind
Chasing flirtatious clouds through the sky
Yet forgetting that in hell
There are still two heavy hearts

Is the God of Love not more than the oars of the heart's boat
Unconsciously disturbing the moon's reflection upon the lake
Yet forgetting that in the waves
There are still two broken hearts

1968

黄昏

我是站在橘红色的礁石上
脚下翻腾着血的波浪
这些感情的波涛沉默着
巨大的悲痛失去了声响

不是躺在爱人的胸旁
也不是睡在朋友的手掌
不！不！我是站在
腐朽精神的白色尸骨上

晚风掀起我的头发
带来童年天真的幻想
头发像是扬起的风帆
带着头颅，又要远航

这儿才是真正的海洋
谁也挣不脱它热情的臂膀
我热烈地亲吻着她
但却跌倒在绿色的山岗

DUSK

I stand on an orange reef
With waves of blood surging beneath
While these waves of feeling fall silent
The bitter grief loses even its sound

Not lying in the arms of a lover
Nor even sleeping on the palm of a friend
No . . . no, I am standing upon
The bleached bones of decomposed spirits

Night winds lift my hair
Inducing the naïve dreams of a child
The hair, raised like a sail,
Leads the head for another voyage

This is the real ocean
No one can break free from her fervent embrace
I kiss her warmly
But fall back upon green ridges

1968

灵魂之一

如果月光象伤透了心的白发
如果星辰象善良真挚的眼睛
那么这灵魂一定是黑夜的宠儿
一定是热烈地爱与恨的结晶

怀着苦思不解的沉重
奔向十字架神秘的阴影
但愿我能看到路口那盏
预示我生命终结的红灯

 ## THE SPIRIT, PART ONE

If moonlight looks like the white hair of a broken heart
If stars appear as sincere and virtuous eyes
Then the spirit is certainly the favorite son of darkness
The crystallization of fervent love and hate

Meditating upon the weight of the obscure
I rush toward the mystical shadow of the crucifix
How I wish I could see the intersection ahead
That red beacon signaling my life's end

1968

希望

多希望你是温暖的阳光
能暖化我心中冻结的冰层
冰雪下还掩埋着有希望的小草
寒风曾折断过它修长的细茎

可你只是匆匆的夕阳
只是一片惨淡的血红
雪水中刚刚挺起身的小草
又将饱经冬夜的寒冷

带着夜间痛苦的泪痕
草儿微笑在淡蓝的黎明
昨天才被暖化的雪水
而今已结成新的冰凌

HOPE

How I hoped you were the warm sun
So that you might thaw me entire
You can still find hopeful grass buried here beneath the ice and snow
Though cold winds have long since broken their slender stems

Yet you are only a hastily setting sun
A sheet of austere bloody red hues
The grass just now pushing up from beneath the slush
Must still endure the cold winter night

Although stained by night's grief
Grass still smiles at daybreak's blue glow
The snow that melted yesterday
Has already formed new icicles

1968

寒风

我来自北方的荒山野林，
和严冬一起在人世降临。
可能因为我粗野又寒冷，
人们对我是一腔的怨恨

为博得人们的好感和亲近，
我慷慨地散落了所有的白银，
并一路狂奔着跑向村舍，
向人们送去丰收的喜讯。

而我却因此成了乞丐，
四处流落，无处栖身。
有一次我试着闯入人家，
却被一把推出窗门。

紧闭的门窗外，人们听任我
在饥饿的晕旋中哀号呻吟。
我终于明白了，在这地球上，
比我冷得多的，是人们的心。

COLD WIND

Coming from the barren mountains and wild forests of the north
I was born amid this world's severe winter
And because I am coarse and wintry
The civilized world fills me with so much resentment

To earn people's intimacy and favor
I generously scatter all of my silver
And run with abandon into the rural villages along the road
To spread news of abundant harvests

Yet this has made a beggar out of me
And now I wander without shelter
Once I tried to barge into someone's home
But was shoved out of the room

On the outside of tightly shut windows and doors, people left me
Starving, barely conscious, I wail and groan
In the end, I understand that in the world
There are people's hearts far colder than me

Summer 1969

给朋友

朋友，你喜欢我的歌
可我只能等心潮退落
在它平坦宽阔的沙滩上
为你寻找一个海螺

我知道你喜欢我的歌
所以我送你一个海螺

朋友，你喜欢我的歌
可我只能等血流缓和
用我绿蓝色的孔雀石静脉
为你铸成一面铜锣

我知道你喜欢我的歌
所以我送你一面铜锣

至于热血沸腾的心窝
和那突突跃动的脉搏
不属于你，也不属于我
她只属于党和祖国

 **FOR A FRIEND**

My friend . . . you like my songs
But I must wait for the tide of my heart to ebb
For only upon a stretch of its smooth, wide beach
Will I be able to search for a shell for you

I know you like my songs
So I want to give you a shell

My friend, you like my songs
Yet I must wait for my blood to slow
So that I can use my green-blue malachite veins
To forge a gong for you

I know you like my songs
So I want to give you a copper gong

As for the passion boiling in my heart*
And my rhythmic, beating pulse
They are neither mine nor yours
But belong to the Party, to the Motherland

Autumn 1969

---

* This line "至于热血沸腾的心窝" is an allusion to the Chinese version of the Communist Internationale.

吹向母亲身边的海风

停一停啊，停一停
吹向母亲身边的海风
请把战士心爱的礼品
送到亲爱的母亲手中

你能吹散黑压压的云层
就一定能带走白云一顶
她安详地在蓝天飘荡
多像渔家扬起的帆蓬

在海防战士的怀抱中
祖国的海洋
是多么安宁
母亲看到了
一定高兴

你能带走暴雨如倾
就一定能捎上海水一捧
把她化作清凉的露水
洒向祖国美好的黎明

在海防战士看来
祖国的每一滴海水
都是这样的晶莹
母亲看到了
一定高兴

去吧，去吧
吹向母亲身边的海风
母亲已经为你
　　　—推开了千山的门户
　　　　打开了万
　　　　家的窗棂

TOWARD MOTHER AN OCEAN WIND BLOWS

Stop, stop, please stop
Toward mother an ocean wind blows
Please send the soldiers' loving gifts
To their adored mother's hands

Now that you can scatter the dark clouds above
You can also bring along the white ones
She quietly flies across the blue sky
Like a fisherman's raised sail

In the coastal soldier's embrace
Is the ocean of the motherland
How incredibly peaceful
If mother could see this
How joyful she would be

Now that you can take away the torrential storm
You can fill both hands with seawater
Transform it into ambrosial dew
And cast it out upon the motherland's fine dawn

In the eyes of the soldiers at sea
Every drop of the motherland's ocean
Is so luminous
If mother could see this
How joyful she would be

Go, please go
Toward mother an ocean wind blows
For you she has already
      —unlocked the gates of a thousand mountains
      and opened the windows of ten thousand houses

December 1972

灵魂之二

假如深夜是我的满头黑发
那么月色便是我一脸倦容
沙沙作响的树丛是我的脚步
晚风便是我漂泊不定的行踪

别去理会白天轻佻的玩笑
不过是一时忘却了内心的苦痛
只有这寂寞的晚上唱出的歌儿
才在揭示我内心深处的伤痕

别去追寻, 我仅仅只有歌声
甚至连歌声也会无影无踪
听到它的人会向后人讲叙
经过人世时, 我脚步放得很轻

 ## THE SPIRIT, PART TWO

If the deep night was the dark hair on my head
Then the moonlight may have been my weary face
If the rustling underbrush was my steps
Then the evening wind was my nomadic traces

Ignore the frivolous jokes of the day
Which are merely a diversion from our inner torments
Only the songs sung in the solitude of night
Can truly reveal the scars lodged in my heart

Don't pursue me, for I have only singing left
And even these sounds would disappear without a trace
Those who listen may tell future generations
When passing through this human world, my steps were
    unbelievably light

Early April 1974

愤怒

我的愤怒不再是泪雨滂沱，
也不是压抑不住的满腔怒火，
更不指望别人来帮我复仇，
尽管曾经有过这样的时刻。

我的愤怒不再是忿忿不平，
也不是无休无止的评理述说，
更不会为此大声地疾呼呐喊，
尽管曾经有过这样的时刻。

虽然我的脸上还带着孩子气，
尽管我还说不上是一个强者，
但是在我未完全成熟的心中，
愤怒已化为一片可怕的沉默。

FURY

My fury is no longer a torrent of tears
Nor an unrestrained fire within my chest
I no longer look to others for vengeance
Even if this was true in the past

My fury is no longer simply a grudge
Nor an endless string of arguments
Less still shouting or screaming
Even if this was true in the past

Although I may look childish
And I cannot claim to be a strong person
In my adolescent heart
My fury has been turned into a terrifying silence

1974

田间休息

我是这样舒适地躺在了
铺满金色阳光的田地里
这是一个难得的片刻
这是紧张劳动的间隙

身旁刚刚被锄掉的小草
还在散发着诱人的香气
旷野上悄悄吹过的风儿
已经给人带来睡意

静静地躺在大地上
伸展开酸懒的肢体
我已把身心全部
都交给了母亲大地

侧过目光向一旁的庄稼望去
枝叶合拢交叉随风摇曳
阳光下随意裁剪着蓝天白云
尽管白云远在，蓝天无际

不远的地方是缓缓流动的渠水
似血液在我脉管里不停冲击
听不到，看不到，但我却感觉得到
一股清凉的渠水流到了心里

我的目光突然盯住
一颗挂在枝叶上的水珠
不清楚是我洒落的汗水
还是颗未被晒干的

她就已经被一阵风儿摇落
很快默默地渗入了松软的土地
不知怎的，我也感到自己
和祖国大地不觉已溶成一体……

RESTING IN THE FIELDS

I am comfortably lying in a field
Covered in a golden hue
This is a singular moment
A distraction from my intense labor

The grass beside me has just been uprooted
And still exudes a delicate fragrance
The winds that have washed the field
Have brought sleep with them

Lying quietly on the ground
Stretching my aching and tired body
I have given myself wholly
To Mother Earth

Look beside the crops
The leaves overlap and sway in the wind
Randomly framing the blue sky, sunlight, and clouds
While the clouds travel far, the blue sky stretches on without end

Water flows smoothly in the nearby trenches
Like blood coursing within my veins
I cannot hear them, I cannot see them, but I can feel
A single thread of cool water flowing from the trenchet lands upon

A clear bead hanging on a leaf
And I am unsure whether it is my own sweat
Or dew not yet evaporated by the sun

She is dislodged by the breeze
And is soon quietly absorbed by the soft earth
Left uncertain, I too feel as if
I am dissolving into my motherland

1977

疯狗

—致奢谈人权的人们

受够无情的戏弄之后，
我不再把自己当人看，
仿佛我成了一条疯狗，
漫无目的地游荡人间。

我还不是一条疯狗，
不必为饥寒去冒风险，
为此我希望成条疯狗，
更深刻地体验生存的艰难。

我还不如一条疯狗！
狗急它能跳出墙院，
而我只能默默地忍受，
我比疯狗有更多的辛酸。

假如我真的成条疯狗
就能挣脱这无情的锁链，
那么我将毫不迟疑地，
放弃所谓神圣的人权。

 **MAD DOG**

—To those who talk sanctimoniously about human rights

After suffering heartless ridicule
It's hard to see myself as human
It's as though I have become a rabid dog
Wandering unrestrained through the world

But I am not yet a rabid dog
Not yet exposed to starvation and the cold
Anyway, I wish I had become this dog
To learn even more about the hardship of existence

Yet I am not as good as a rabid dog!
It would jump these walls if forced
But I can only endure silence
My life holds far fewer choices

If I could really become this dog
I would break free from these indifferent chains
I would not hesitate for a moment
To leave behind so-called sacred human rights

1978

北京的安徽女佣

近年来就在我们的北京，
在比较富裕的家庭当中，
都有可能发生下面，
我要讲述的很平常的事情。

饭后她一边收拾碗筷和板凳，
一边把剩下的菜汤一口喝净。
　别笑，要知道这位从灾区
　刚刚到北京的安徽女佣，
　在家连白薯干都吃不上，
　又怎见得到这一点油星。

你的宝贝舒适地依偎在她前胸，
被她轻轻摇晃着哄入梦境。
　你可曾想到她亲生的孩子，
　一个同样可爱的小生命，
　竟在去年遭灾的情况下，
　愣这么饿死在她的怀中。

她不大注重你们的眼色，
不在乎睡在过道和厨房中。
拿到工钱她小心地攒起，
一分不花地寄回家中。

盼到家信，她请你们
一字不落地读给她听，
你若留心她眼角的泪水，
便看到她那质朴的心灵。

在此时此地，看此情此景，
我心中久久不能平静。
于是向致力于改革的青年们
讲述了这件很平常的事情。

ANHUI MAID IN BEIJING

These days in our Beijing
Things like this can happen
In the wealthier families
So this is a common story

As she cleaned up, packed the bowls, chopsticks, and chairs after dinner
She finished up the leftover soup in a single mouthful
    Don't laugh, she was a refugee
    A maid from Anhui who had just arrived in Beijing
    She had not so much as a sweet potato at home
    Or even the smallest drop of oil

Your baby is lying comfortably upon her chest
As she gently rocks him into his dreaming world
    Have you ever thought about her child
    The gentle living being, as lovely as your own
    Who in last year's flood
    Starved to death in her arms

She doesn't care about the looks she receives
And doesn't mind sleeping in the hallway or kitchen
When she gets her pay, she carefully tucks it away
To be sent back home, without spending a penny

Excitedly receiving a letter from home, she asks you
To read each and every word
If you paid attention to the tears welling up in the corners of her eyes
You could see straight into her simple soul

Right here and now, look at this situation
My heart cannot stay calm for long
So for the young, who devote themselves to reform,
I have told this common story

December 8, 1979

热爱生命

也许我瘦弱的身躯象攀附的葛藤，
把握不住自己命运的前程，
那请在凄风苦雨中听我的声音，
仍在反复地低语：热爱生命。

也许经过人生激烈的搏斗后，
我死得比那湖水还要平静。
那请去墓地寻找的我的碑文，
上面仍刻着：热爱生命。

我下决心：用痛苦来做砝码，
我有信心：以人生做为天秤。
我要称出一个人生命的价值，
要后代以我为榜样：热爱生命。

的确，我十分珍爱属于我的
那条曲曲弯弯的荒草野径，
正是通过这条曲折的小路，
我才认识到如此艰辛的人生。

我流浪儿般的赤着双脚走来，
深感到途程上顽石棱角的坚硬，
再加上那一丛丛拦路的荆棘
使我每一步都留下一道血痕。

我乞丐似地光着脊背走去，
深知道冬天风雪中的饥饿寒冷，
和夏天毒日头烈火一般的灼热，
这使我百倍地珍惜每一丝温情。

但我有着向命运挑战的个性，
虽是屡经挫败，我绝不轻从。
我能顽强地活着，活到现在，
就在于：相信未来，热爱生命。

LOVE LIFE

If my emaciated body looks like a climbing vine
That cannot grasp its own destiny
Then please listen to my voice in the bleak rain and wind
A deep murmur keeps saying: love life

If after the fierce battles of life
My death arrives more placid than the surface of a lake
Then please search the cemetery for my epitaph
And carve into stone: love life

I have made my decision—let pain be the weight
Yes, I am certain—let my life be the scale
I will weigh life's value
To let my descendants follow my example: love life

Indeed, I truly treasure the crooked grass-covered path
Which belongs to the wild
As it is upon this winding road
That I have known my difficult life

Like a young vagabond, I walk shoeless
Feel each sharp stone along the road
The thorns that have obstructed my way
Have marked every step with my blood

Like a beggar, I walk with nothing on my back
Fully aware of the cold and hunger of winter snow
And the poisoned heat of the summer sun
So I cherish every thread of gentle warmth

Yet I have an obstinate mind
And though beaten time and again, I will not stay down
But stand up and keep moving on
For I believe in the future and love life

1979

也许

也许你是我的月亮
你不要躲进乌黑的云层
请你为我在茫茫夜色里
照亮人生坎坷的路程

也许你是我的太阳
请帮我驱散心头的寒冷
我还能找回逝去的青春
和我年轻时代的热情

也许你只是我的启明星
只把我从睡梦中唤醒
让我在黑暗中苦苦思索
而你却悄悄地躲进了黎明

也许你根本不属于我
这也在我的意料当中
像石块被随意扔进了湖水
无意间打破了我的平静

PERHAPS

Perhaps you are my moon
So don't hide behind the dark clouds
I beg you in the endless night
To light the difficult journey ahead

Perhaps you are my sun
Please help me dispel the cold gathering within
I can still retrieve my spent youth
And its lost passions

Perhaps you are merely Venus
Who has woken me from my dreams
Leaving me to wonder in the dark
While you silently fade into the dawn

Perhaps you do not belong to me at all
I suspect this is so
Like a stone randomly tossed into a lake
You accidentally broke into my tranquility

September 9, 1980

我爱之一

我爱峻峭挺拔的山峰
能使我更接近光辉的太阳
更爱山间崎岖的小路
能引起我对人生的联想

我爱波涛澎湃的大海
她像生活一样地动荡
更爱海上孤独的白帆
得意或失神地在海面徜徉

我爱难以驯服的江河
像我多年来对命运的反抗
更爱欢快清澈的小溪
她使我回味童年的时光

我爱辽阔无际的原野
五谷丰登，丰收在望
更爱狭小窄短的稿纸
收藏着丰富的精神食粮

我爱蓝天上漂泊的白云
她多像我年轻时的模样
更爱乌云间沉闷的雷声
那是现在我心中的鸣响

I LOVE, PART ONE

I love the lofty sheer mountain peaks
That bring me closer to the burning sun
But I love the rugged mountain roads even more
As they stir my thoughts on life

I love the ocean of surging waves
She rises and falls like life
But I love the lonely white sails even more
Whether proud or dejected, they sail across the surface of the sea

I love unconquered rivers
They are like my own long struggle against the fates
But I love the joyous clear stream even more
She reminds me of my childhood

I love the vast expanse of endless fields
Which will produce abundant harvests of every crop
But I love the narrow and short sheets of draft paper even more
As they store rich provisions for the mind

I love the white cloud lingering in the sky
She looks so much like me when I was young
But I love the rumbling thunder of dark clouds even more
As this is the call reverberating in my heart

December 5, 1980

遐想

（此诗又名《小帆船》）

一只小帆船
搁浅在沙滩
紧紧依偎在
大海的身边

难道真是金色海滩上的平静
竟使它如此地沉醉迷恋
不，是它身边的微风细浪
卷不走它，它无法归还

但它深信，终究有一天
风暴会把它带回海面
它那宁折不弯的桅杆上
将会再次升起风帆

享受一下海水的咸苦，风浪的惊险
就是被撞得粉身碎骨
只要是葬身海底，它毫无怨言
终究算是了却了平生的夙愿

一只小小的帆船
搁浅在大海身边
微风带起细浪
轻轻扣着船舷

 ## REVERIE

("Small Sailboat")

A small, small sailboat
Lands on the beach
Leaning down
Upon the shore side

Was it the calmness of golden sands
That seduced it so?
No, the gentle wind and fine waves
Cannot carry it away, cannot return it to the sea

Yet it believes there will be a day
When the storm will bring it back to the sea
Its mast, which would rather break than bend,
Will raise its sails one more time

Enjoy the bitter saltwater and the danger of the storm
Even if it is smashed into shards
As long as it's buried deep beneath the sea, it will not complain
For this would fulfill its long-awaited dream

A small, small sailboat
Lands upon the beach
Gentle winds push slight waves
Softly against the small ship's side

November 24, 1981

愿望

我曾经有一个美好的愿望
把秋天的原野裁成纸张
用红的高粱,黄的稻谷
写下五彩斑斓的诗章

可是没等收完庄稼
我的手稿已满目荒凉
只在狂暴的风雪过后
白纸上才留下脚印数行

 ## FANTASY

I once had a beautiful dream
In which I cut an open autumn field into sheets of paper
With red sorghum and unhusked brown rice
I wrote out poems in every color

Yet before the harvest is over
My manuscript already lies barren
Only after a raging snowstorm
Will lines of footprints appear across the blank paper

1983

人生之一

经历了世态炎凉的人生战场
使我深受了难以愈合的内伤
当欢欣和伤感的泪水串成诗句
就有了闪光的字句，精彩的诗章

的确，我曾奋斗，消沉，探索
像同时代的一个普通的人一样
只是我是在诗歌的道路上奔波——
这一切现已成为最珍贵的宝藏

今天，我默默地读着这些诗行
发现她还是那么令人神往——
这时，我只有一个最简单的要求
让我一个人先静静地独自品尝

 **LIFE, PART ONE**

I have survived the rise and fall of life's battlefield
And I have sustained internal injuries that will never heal
But when the tears of joy and grief fall
Glimmering words and brilliant poems will arise

Indeed, I've struggled, depressed but pressing on
Like everybody else, like an ordinary person
But I have pressed forward on the path of poetry
Which has become my most valuable property

Today I calmly read these lines
And find them as fascinating as ever
Yet at this moment I have only a simple favor
Let me quietly savor them alone

1984

我爱之二

我爱花朵凋零后的果实
茁壮地成长在枝枝中央
虽没有迷人的芬芳和色彩
却朴实地扫尽了浮华的感伤

我爱夏日暴雨的前奏
雷电点燃了灵感的火光
前有难以忍耐的烦闷
后有淋漓尽致的酣畅

我爱深秋金黄的枯叶
任寒风采摘，簌簌飘降
凄风苦雨中忍受着践踏
默默无私地献身于土壤

我爱数九的白雪茫茫
给贫瘠的土地以丰收的希望
并深深地向劳累了一年的人们
预祝着来年的如意吉祥

 **I LOVE, PART TWO**

I love the fruit that follows withered flowers
As it grows strong upon the branches
It may not possess enchanting fragrances or colors
But it sweeps away vain desires

I love the prelude to a strong summer rainstorm
Lightning ignites the very fire of inspiration
Unbearable agony appears before it
Afterward, torrential sublimity

I love the withered leaves of late autumn
Ready for the cold wind to send them tumbling
Withstanding the trampling of cold wind and rain
They dissolve into the soil without a sound

I love the endless snow of deep winter
Carrying hope of harvests to a barren land
For weary laborers who have worked the year through
It renews hope and good luck for the seasons to come

1984

黎明的海洋

西面黑夜的背影是那么寒酸
东方黎明的心胸是那样坦荡
一群群海鸟在向大海呼喊
已是黎明时分，醒来吧海洋

醒来吧，醒来吧，黑色的海洋
你承受着黑夜的压抑
你深感到黑暗的窒息
你肌肉的每一次抽搐
都是一道寒心的波浪

海风鼓起你剧烈起伏的胸膛
你强劲的呼吸掀起滔天巨浪
一次又一次地冲淡着黑夜的劣迹
天空才有了一线朦朦的亮光……

海鸟在用尖厉的呼叫
报告着黑夜最后的抵抗
正匆匆把明星的银币
草草收入自己的私囊
黑夜正在准备逃亡

终于醒来了，黑色的海洋
赤裸着肌肉闪光的臂膀
在那天边的海平线上
奋力托起了火红的太阳……

大概海洋也受了伤——
不然怎么会有
一摊殷红的鲜血
浮荡在黎明的海面上？！

☀ THE OCEAN AT DAWN

The dark outline of the west looks so worn down from behind
In the east the broad mind of dawn stretches on without end
Flocks of seabirds call out to the sea
It's already daybreak; wake up, ocean

Wake, wake up, dark ocean
You have endured the oppression of night
And have felt the long asphyxiation of darkness
Every anxious twitch of yours
Is an ice-cold wave

The sea winds lift your heaving chest
Your deep breaths raise monstrous waves
To weaken the wrongdoings of the night, again and again
The sky finally reveals the barest hint of light . . .

The seabirds call out shrilly
Reporting on the dark night's final resistance
It stashes the silver coin of the stars
Hastily in its dark purse
Ready to flee

It's finally awake, the dark ocean
Naked arms, luminous muscle
On the horizon at the edge of the sky
Struggling to raise the fire-red sun . . .

Perhaps the ocean is also injured—
If not, how
Would this red pool of blood
Float upon its skin at dawn?!

July 18, 1985

大地和落叶的对话

落叶说:"为了寻根,我才飘落
轻轻地,不曾损伤了什么
可人们却仍在我身上随意践踏
竟然让我受这般的摧残和折磨。"

"你看,在我身上一切都在成长
而我呢,"大地说,"却日益贫困瘠薄
看来你终究还知道点什么是幸福
不然你的话语怎么这样尖刻?!"

落叶不再说什么
我却明白了许多

DIALOGUE BETWEEN THE GROUND AND A FALLEN LEAF

Fallen Leaf: "I have fallen, softly,
Without harm, to find my root
Yet people continue to walk upon me as they please
And I suffer as I am destroyed"

"Just look, all things grow upon me
Yet I," said the earth, "become less fertile by the day
It would seem you know little about true happiness
Otherwise what you said to me would not cut so deeply"

The fallen leaf spoke no more
But I had come to understand

July 27, 1985

无题

星辰似我热切的目光
月亮像你苍白的脸庞
我们紧紧地依偎在一起
手握着手儿久久不放

你对我温柔委婉地叙说
如优美的旋律在耳边回响
我只有笨拙地"嗯嗯"的回答
像不时敲打的节拍一样

也许你会觉得我此刻深沉
许久一言不发，像莫测的海洋
其实倒还不如说我浅薄
竟找不出准确的语言表达思想……

 **UNTITLED**

Stars appear as my fervent eyes
The moon, your pale face
We lean so close together
Our hands remain clasped

You speak so gently to me
Like a beautiful melody so close to my ear
I can only answer by stupidly mumbling
As if marking a beat in time

Perhaps you think I look deep
Wordless, like a depthless ocean
But I am so shallow
I cannot find the right words to say . . .

July 1985

枯叶

我随手拾起一片枯叶
若有所思地仔细端详

　　干瘪的叶片上皱纹深藏
　　背面叶脉像青筋暴涨
　　没有金黄荣耀的色泽
　　只是一张青灰色的面庞

　　它曾是那么丰满光亮
　　墨绿的叶片闪耀着希望
　　风暴中有它激烈的争辩
　　骄阳下遮片舒适的荫凉

　　而今, 在命运寒流的驱赶下
　　却像个卖艺的老人一样
　　蜷缩着身躯沿街流落
　　瑟瑟发抖的低吟浅唱

一片无人理睬的枯叶
却使我心中一片迷惘

 **DEAD LEAF**

Picking up a dead leaf close at hand
I examine it closely, deep in thought

    Deep wrinkles hide on the dry leaf
    The nerves that run its length swell like blue veins
    It has no color of gold or glory
    Only a pale gray face

    It was luminous, full
    Its future used to shimmer on its dark green
    But storms shook it in a furious contest
    And the scorching sun blocked its comfortable shade

    Now, driven by the cold currents of fate,
    It is like an old performer
    Bent over, wandering the streets
    Shivering and chanting deeply

A single fragment of an ignored leaf
Leaves me confounded

November 1985

人生之二

暴雨后我践踏着片片残红
纯真和希望也破碎在泥水中
骄阳暴雨和我一起
糟蹋了年青人最可贵的感情

秋雨低泣着，面对满地
残枝败叶，落英枯藤
可带着来年希望的种子
已落在这肥沃的心田之中

风雪狂笑着，一夜抹去
大地身上胭脂的污痕
留下个清新纯朴的世界
这正是我所面对的人生

 ## LIFE, PART TWO

After a storm I trample red fragmented flowers
Innocence and hope have fallen to pieces in the mud
And together with the burning sun and driving rain
I have destroyed the most precious emotion of youth

Weeping, the autumn rain looks down upon the ground
Covered in broken limbs, leaves, vines
Yet the seeds of next year's hope
Already grow within the fertile soil of the heart

Wind and snow laugh wildly through the night
Erasing the rouge stains on the ground
Only a natural, innocent world is left
This is the life I face ahead

November 1985

诗人的桂冠

诗人的桂冠和我毫无缘分
我是为了记下欢乐和痛苦的一瞬
即使我已写下那么多诗行
不过我看它们不值分文

我是人们啐在地上的痰迹
不巧会踏上哪位姑娘的 足印*
我看这决不是为了沾上我
一定是出于无意决非真心

我是我那心灵圣殿的墙上
孩子们刻下的污秽的字文
岁月再长也不会被抹去
但对这颗高傲的心却丝毫无损

人们会问你到底是什么
是什么都行但不是诗人
只是那些不公正的年代里
一个无足轻重的牺牲品

---

* The character ji (4th tone) 迹 has been changed to yin (4th tone) 印. While the
meaning of the line remains the same, the sound has changed.

 ## THE POET'S LAUREL

The laurel of a poet wasn't in the stars for me
I serve only to record the instant of joy and grief
And even if I have written many poems
They are not worth a penny

I am the spit on the ground
That happened to fall into a girl's footprint
I imagine she does not want to touch me
But does so wholly by chance

On the temple walls of my soul, I am
The graffiti carved by children
That will not be erased for years to come
But it cannot damage this proud heart

People would ask me who the hell I am
I can be anyone but a poet
I exist in this unjust age
A nobody, an insignificant victim

1986, in the mental institution

受伤的心灵

时光白白流逝的惶恐
时时惊吓着我的魂灵
我心中还有希望的花朵
可无聊像条蛇缠绕着枝藤

我的心灵已无法挣脱
能向谁发出求救的呼声
我只有白天廉价的欢乐
可廉价的欢乐是苦闷的象征

不得已，我敞开自己的心胸
让你看看这受伤的心灵——
上面到处是磕开的酒瓶盖
和戳灭烟头时留下的疤痕

MY INJURED SOUL

The terror of passing time
Often frightens my spirit
Hope may still bloom within
But boredom twists like snakes around its vine

My soul is not able to break loose
And there is no one to call out to
All I have are the cheap pleasures of the day
But these are the signs of my blues

Having little choice, I open my chest
To let you see my injured soul
Which is scattered by cast-off bottle lids
And scars left by stamping out cigarettes

October 20, 1987

秋意

秋雨读着落叶上的诗句,
经秋风选送,寄给了编辑,
那绿叶喧哗的青春时代,
早装订成册为精美的诗集。

有一片秋叶竟飘进我心里,
上面还带着晶莹的泪滴,
款款落在我胸中的旷野,
伏在我心头上低声抽泣。

辨别得出,是你的泪水,
苦苦的,咸咸的,挺有诗意,
可滴在我心中未愈合的伤口上,
却是一阵阵痛心的回忆。

THE CHILL OF AUTUMN

The autumn rain recites the poems on the fallen leaves
Selecting which ones to send to the editor
Periods of new growth filled with the clamor of green leaves
Have already been bound into an exquisite collection of poems

A single autumn leaf unexpectedly floats into my heart
With crystal tears above
It gently falls upon the open field of my chest
Bends over my heart and quietly weeps

I can discern the nature of your tears
Their salt, their bitterness, their poetry
But those that fall upon the unhealed wounds in my heart
Are but fits of grieving memory

1987

我不知道

我不知道，我可真的不知道，
为何偏爱冬夜中的寒风衰草，
是因为衰草可令人随意践踏，
还是寒风能给人清醒的思考？

随意踱步能使人浮想联翩，
冬夜里内心中跳跃着诗意的火苗，
喧嚣不安的白天得不到的东西，
我要在冰冷的月波中细细寻找。

我不知道，我可真的不知道，
何时嘴角才有了得意的微笑——
直到灵感化为动人的诗句，
才感到已是寒气逼人的拂晓……

 **I DON'T KNOW**

I don't know, I really don't know
Why I prefer the cold wind and dead grass of a winter's night
Is it because dead grass can be trampled at will
Or is it that cold wind brings me sober thoughts?

Walking aimlessly, thoughts flood my mind
And the flame of poetry flickers in my heart during the coldest night
For those things that cannot be found by day
I will seek out under the moon's frozen wave

I don't know, I really don't know
When the corners of my mouth will turn toward a self-satisfied smile—
For this will only happen when inspiration is transformed into good
    lines
Only then will I feel the cold day begin to break . . .

1987

向青春告别

别了，青春
那通宵达旦的狂饮

如今打开泡药材的酒瓶
小心地斟满八钱的酒盅
然后一点一滴地品位着
稍稍带些苦味的人生

别了，青春
那争论时喷吐的烟云

依然是一支接一支地点燃
很快的度过漫长的一天
不同在，愿意守着片宁静
虽说，孤独却也轻松

别了，青春
那骄阳下，暴雨中的我们

七分的聪明被用于圆滑的处世
终于导致名利奸污了童贞
挣到了舒适还觉得缺少了点什么
是因为丧失了灵魂，别了，青春。

 **FAREWELL TO YOUTH**

Farewell, youth
And drinking heavily through the night

Nowadays alcohol bottles are filled with medicine
Carefully poured into one-ounce shots
Then taste sip by sip
Life's slight bitterness

Farewell, youth
And cigarette smoke billowing above our arguments

Now I still light up one after another
And the long days pass rapidly by
But I would rather remain tranquil
Though lonely, life's not difficult

Farewell, youth
And the time we walked under rainstorms and scorching sun

We wasted seventy percent of our intelligence keeping up slick
    appearances
Yet in the end, fame and money stole our virginity
Comfort may be secured from labor, but something's missing
For we have lost our selves, we have bid farewell to youth

1989

在精神病院

为写诗我情愿搜尽枯肠
可喧闹的病房怎苦思冥想
开粗俗的玩笑，妙语如珠
提起笔竟写不出一句诗行

有时止不住想发泄愤怒
可那后果却不堪设想……
天呵，为何一次又一次地
让我在疯人院消磨时光！

………………………………
………………………………
………………………………
………………………………

当惊涛骇浪从心头退去
心底只剩下空旷与凄凉……
怕别人看见噙泪的双眼
我低头踱步，无事一样

 **IN THE ASYLUM**

I would rather exhaust my mind to find poetry
But I can't rack my brains here in this grating ward
Hearing vulgar jokes and clever quips
I can't write even a single line

At times rage wells up and teeters on the edge of expression
But the consequences would be inconceivable
God! Why time and again
Am I forced to waste my days in this insane asylum!

....
....
....
....

When the stormy waves recede from my mind
In my heart only emptiness and desolation remain
I fear that others might see my eyes welling up with tears
So I look down, and stroll away as if nothing had happened

May 12–21, 1991, in the Beijing No. 3 Welfare House

归宿

由于创作生命的短促
诗人的命运吉凶难卜
为迎接灵感危机的挑战
我不怕有任何更高的代价付出

优雅的举止和贫寒的窘迫
曾给了我不少难言的痛楚
但终于我的诗行方阵的大军
跨越了精神死亡的峡谷

埋葬弱者灵魂的坟墓
绝对不是我的归宿

一片杂草丛生的荒坟
坟头仅仅是几抔黄土
这就是我祖祖辈辈的陵园
长年也无人看管守护

活着的时候倍尝艰辛
就连死后也如此凄苦
我激动地热泪夺眶而出
一阵风带来奶奶的叮嘱

"人生一世，草木一秋，
孩子，这是你最后的归宿。"

 THE FINAL RETURN

Because the life of creativity is so brief
A poet never knows what his future holds
To prepare for the crisis of inspiration's passing
I'm not afraid to pay any price

Being refined yet embarrassed by my poverty
Causes more suffering than I can say
Yet in the end my lines of poetry are a formidable force
Able to vault the chasm of my own spiritual death

For I will not return home
To a tomb for weak spirits

A desolate tomb overgrown with weeds
Unmarked mounds covered with sand
This is my family's ancestral graveyard
Left untended for so many years

They led such difficult lives
And became even more miserable after death
Moved, I cannot hold back my tears
As a strong wind brings my grandmother's warning:

"People have but one life, and grass but one fall
My child, this will be your final destination"

1991, in the Beijing No. 3 Welfare House

你

寂寞时你又一次
闯入我的心灵

我在心里呼唤你的名字
脑际不断闪过你的身影
因为你代表着我的青年时代
那时爱你爱得那样深情

之后，命运给了你那么多不公正
可回首往事你却谈笑风生

寂寞时你又一次
闯入我的心灵

终于你走了过来步履轻盈
老了些相貌穿着还那样普通
象一枝花期早已开过的玫瑰
甚至仿佛连绿叶也已凋零

面对未来人生严峻的提问
你的回答始终是那样真诚

寂寞时你又一次
闯入我的心灵

YOU

When I find myself lonely
You storm right into me

My heart keeps calling your name
Your shadow keeps flashing through my mind
Because you represent my youth
When I loved you so completely

In the end, fate dealt you an unfair hand
Yet looking back, you talk as if nothing happened

When I find myself lonely
You storm right into me

Finally, your swaying figure approaches
Older, you appear so ordinary
Like a rose whose bloom is already spent
Even your green leaves have withered away

Facing the grim questions ahead
You always answer them with unyielding sincerity

And when I find myself alone
You storm right into me

1991, in the Beijing No. 3 Welfare House

我的青春

正值我生命中朝气蓬勃的春天
遇到了冰和铁的时代特有的心寒
我一腔青春热血被冰冻三尺
忧郁的心情化作了首首诗篇

像洁白的雪片熄灭了红色的火焰
黑灰色的柴堆上腾起一缕青烟
…………
…………

 **MY YOUTH**

In the flourishing spring of life
I met the discontentment of the era of iron and ice
The young blood in my chest froze
As my dark thoughts became poems

Like flames extinguished by a new-fallen snow
From a dark gray pile of firewood rises a twisting thread of smoke
. . .
. . .

April 1994

诗作

白天，荒漠的戈壁滩上
没有一丝云彩遮挡
沙石滚烫，热风扑面———
直抒胸臆的是烈日骄阳

夜晚，内心一片荒芜
笑骂嬉怒，我无拘无束
眼底收尽了千古悲凉
肆无忌惮的诗留纸上

 **POETRY**

At day in the Gobi Desert
Not even a cloud for shelter
Sand and rock burn and wind scorches my face
The blazing sun expresses itself without restraint

At night my inner landscape lies empty
Laughter, shame, joy, and rage all fly out unchecked
Surveying the horizon of a thousand barren years
I write my unbridled poetry on the page

September 26, 1994

人生之三

寒雨冷落了争奇斗艳的姿容
把难堪的角色给了攀附的葛藤
秋风一扫满地的残枝败叶
鸟语花香已成了昨日梦境

厌倦了姑娘们难以满足的好奇
听烦了朋友们令人不安的吹捧
大红大紫的喧嚣如此收场
不管对谁都是个绝妙的嘲讽

面对严峻的现实出奇地冷静
面向理想的未来仍一片真诚
每前进一步付出的泪滴汗水
是那么晶莹令人感叹不平

 **LIFE, PART THREE**

Cold rain raises a cold shoulder to the stunning flowers
Leaving the ingratiating wisteria embarrassed
Once the autumn wind swept away the broken limbs and leaves
Bird songs and fragrant blooms have receded into yesterday's dream

Exhausted by the insatiable curiosity of girls
Annoyed by the uncomfortable flattery of friends
The excitement of fame vanishes into this
One final, if brilliant, joke

Remaining sober in the face of life's harsh reality
Yet still committed to an ideal future
Every drop of sweat and tears I shed at each step
Is so clear as to invite the pity of others

1994

诗人命苦

孤独地跋涉人生旅途
看透红尘才略有所悟
诗人命苦，当夜深人静
地下天上才辟条大路

一阵恍惚如青云平步
有流星划过似走笔不俗
不虚度此生，有白纸黑字——
惊人之作，我一笔呼出！

 **A POET'S BITTER FATE**

Alone, trudging the journey of life
Only by seeing through this secular world might one begin to
    understand
The bitter life of a poet, and only in the dead of the night
Can he open up a smooth, wide path across heaven and earth

As if in a trance, I pace the clouds
A meteor streaks across the sky and awakens my inspiration
One must not waste life with black ink upon white paper
Miraculous poem, written in one breath!

April 1995

对家乡的祝愿

鲁西南那片肥田沃土
掩埋着多少先烈的忠骨
村寨前那静静的流水淌着
我祖祖辈辈的血汗泪珠

祝愿这片古老的土地上
稻花飘香麦浪起伏
祝愿那养育了我的乳汁
汩汩不断,永不干涸

愿乡间年年敲响丰收的锣鼓
愿年下总有人家聘姑娘娶媳妇
奉劝爷儿们少抽口低劣的纸烟
就是喝多了也不要那么粗鲁

愿夏收麦场上,冬天炉火边再困
也强撑着听老辈人谈今说古的孩子们
能如愿以偿地找到传说中丢失的
那把永远倒不干的神奇的酒壶

再有就是乡间的那条小路
我从小就在这坎坷中摔打学步
真诚地祝愿这条路上能走出
一代代家乡的栋梁,社会的脊骨

思恋着乡亲,怀念着故土
这就是身在异乡的我
跪拜在家乡父老面前
对乡亲们道一声深深的祝福

A BLESSING FOR MY HOME

In the rich soil of southwestern Shandong
Countless martyrs are buried
In the quiet stream before the village
Flows the ancestral sacrifice of generations

Bless this ancient earth
Wafting aroma of rice and undulating waves of wheat
Bless this nourishing milk
Endlessly flowing, never drying up

Bless the gongs of the countryside that sound the harvest every year
And let there always be engagements and weddings at year's end
I hope friends will smoke fewer low-quality cigarettes
And be kind even when they're drunk

Bless the barley fields of summer, and being close to the stove in winter
And children who fight off sleep a moment longer to hear the old-
    timer's stories
Filling their dreams with that which cannot be found
The legendary wine pot that never runs dry

And then there is the country road where
I fell so many times before I learned to walk
Let this road guide generations of people
To become the pillar of the hometown and the backbone of society

I so long for my home, my family
This is me . . . in a strange land
I kneel deeply before the people of my homeland
To bless them with everything I still have

1995

想到过去

过去的事情一时记忆不详
只记得那时迷恋在艺术的殿堂
一个多么令人着迷的世界
令人着迷,令人着迷得发狂

茶饭不进的白天和失眠的夜晚
一首小诗便找回了所有的补偿
然后娓娓动听地向朋友颂读
得到的反响是一片惊叹和赞扬

可就在这忘乎一切的同时
又在悄悄酝酿下一篇诗章
就这样构成了我的青年时代——
谁知一想到过去,竟如此辉煌

THINKING OF THE PAST

I've forgotten almost everything
Only the memory of being entranced by arts' gallery remains
What a spellbinding world
So enchanting, its rapture may very well be the rupture of sanity itself

Days without a meal or even tea, and nights without sleep
Yet a single poem could make up for the hardship
Afterward I chant it deeply to my friends
Who respond with a jubilant reception

But at the moment I become delirious with joy
The next poem begins its own quiet gestation
Such events make up for the days of my youth
Who knew that looking back would be so wonderful

March 5, 1996

欲望

从加冕"著名"两字肉麻地相互捧场
到金钱的诱惑令人心寒地横冲直撞
学术界之中不带脸红的自我吹嘘
明显地是在提高自己身价的分量

在利令智昏得令人恐慌的时候
丑恶公开地在人生舞台亮相
欲望，到处是压抑不住的冲动——
这市场上最不值钱的叫得最响

GREED

"Fame" is bestowed by each upon the other with nauseating flattery
And the lust for money forces its way without mercy
Academics sing their own praises without blushing
Everyone is obsessed with their own upward mobility

When people are blinded by their lust for more
And flaunt their repulsive wealth in public
Greed spreads through the world unchecked—
And in this marketplace the cheapest ideas have the loudest
  reverberations

June 25, 1996

雨夜

细细分辨静夜的雨声
之中有雨打阔叶的沉重
不乏入地难辨的细微
夹杂着碰撞硬物的破碎

眼前漆黑，只闻大雨瓢泼
偶有闪电划过照亮山河
才见地上的一切都镀层水银——
想象得出是幅极精彩的水墨

那如低音背景的一片茫茫
那咫尺之间房檐下清脆的声响
那夜幕，那静，那冷冷清清，无疑
是一首最易带人入境的乐章

细细分辨着雨声
品味着诗意人生……

RAINY NIGHT

Listen carefully to the different sounds of the rain against the
    silence of night
The heavy rhythm upon broad leaves
The nearly imperceptible sound of it vanishing into the soil
Infused with the clatter of rain against harder things

Before the eyes is only darkness, only the sounds of heavy rain
Yet lightning at times illuminates the rivers and mountains
Revealing a ground of flowing mercury
The ghostly landscape of an ink-wash painting can hardly be imagined

The boundless void set in the bass voice
Crisp ringing sounding from beneath nearby eaves
The curtain of night is a deep silence, its chill an unwavering presence
And the movement of the orchestra a gate through which we enter

Listen gently, carefully, to the different sounds of the rain
And quietly taste the life of this poetic season . . .

July 31, 1996

我这样写歌

这首小诗完成的一刻
结束了一场精神的折磨
别错以为我不修边幅
其实我早已失魂落魄

没人能理解你此时的心境
没有人倾听你真诚的述说
也没有朋友赶来相聚
喝一杯,以得到一时的解脱

清茶一杯,自斟自酌
生活清苦算不得什么
最怕感情的大起大落后
一个人承受心灵的寂寞

年年如此,日月如梭
远离名利也远离污浊
就这样在荒凉僻静的一角
我写我心中想唱的歌

痛苦对人们无一例外
对诗人尤其沉重尖刻
孤独向我的笔力挑战——
心儿颤抖着,我写歌

THIS IS HOW I WRITE MY SONGS

The moment a short poem is complete
Marks the end of my mind's torment
Don't misjudge my unkempt appearance
I have long since been driven to distraction

No one understands your mind in this moment
No one wants to listen to your true story
None of your friends rush to be with you
To have a drink and a laugh or two

An ordinary cup of tea, poured and sipped alone
It doesn't really matter that I am poor and lonely
I simply fear that after the rise and fall of love
One has to endure his solitude alone

Nothing changes year after year; time flies past
I try to avoid vanity and vulgarity
Seeking silence in a quiet, desolate corner
I write the songs I want to sing

Everyone suffers, everyone does
But a poet far more keenly
When solitude challenges my imagination
I write my songs with a trembling heart

March 12, 1997

当你老了

当你老了，已经步履蹒跚，
身后是你走过的万里山川。
有你失足的令人心寒的山谷，
也有你爬起又登上的艺术峰巅。

当你老了，梦中常见大海，
你就是船长又驶出平静的港弯。
继续在人生苦海中乘风破浪，
你比年轻时更加沉着勇敢。

当你老了，心境十分坦然，
昏花的老眼时常傲视着篮天。
仿佛在问：有谁像你一样
历经磨难 写那些苦难的诗篇……

 **WHEN YOU ARE OLD**

When you are old and cumbersome
A thousand mountains and planes lie behind you
As do ruinous valleys you once fell into
The pinnacles of art already summited

When you are old, you continually dream of the sea
You feel like a captain sailing away from peaceful harbors one more
    time
To continue braving the winds and waves of life's seas
Yet calmer and braver now than when you were young

When you are old, your mind becomes tranquil
Dim-sighted, you proudly watch the sky again and again
As if asking: are there others like you
Suffering but still writing their own poems of tribulation . . .

1997

在精神病福利院的八年

盛夏如雨的汗滴下擦拭楼道
隆冬刺骨的冷水中洗净饭碗
只有在支撑着困倦苦思的长夜
一丝温暖的春意才遣上笔端

懒惰，自私，野蛮和不卫生的习惯……
在这里集中了中国人所有的弱点
这一切如残忍无情的铁砧，工锤
击打得我精神的火花四溅

一下便把我的周身点燃
此时我旺盛的生命力像一束
燃烧得噼啪作响的火焰
而思绪却像一缕轻烟……

不因没成为栋梁的树干
而感到哪怕是一点点的遗憾
在物欲像漫天风雪的冬夜
我情愿为一堆作柴草的枝蔓

点燃它，给赶路人以光亮
让饥寒受冻者来取暖
而我将化为灰烬
被一阵狂风吹散

EIGHT YEARS IN A PSYCHIATRIC WARD

I scrub the stairways in summer as sweat falls like rain
And wash rice bowls in winter with biting cold water
Only in the long nights, when I try to endure endless fatigue,
Does the meager warmth of spring fill my pen

Sloth, selfishness, crudeness, unsanitary habits . . .
All the weaknesses of the Chinese people are concentrated here
Together they become a brutal hammer on an anvil
Smashing my mind into a shower of sparks

In an instant setting me aflame
And at that moment my life, its very vitality,
Is like a bouquet of crackling flames
And my thoughts a single strand of smoke . . .

I am not ashamed in the slightest
Of having not grown into the tree used as the center beam
For in the winter night, when materialism spreads like rushing wind
 and snow,
I would rather be a sprig of kindling

Ignite this wood, and offer its light to those who are hungry and cold
Its warmth to those in need
Even as I will vanish into ash
And disappear in the wind

March 3, 1998

生涯的午后

冬日的太阳已缓缓西沉
但温暖如旧，更加宜人
有生涯午后成就的辉煌
谁去想半生的勤奋和郁闷

冬日的斜阳还那么斯斯文文
天边已渐渐涌上厚厚的阴云
注定又有一场冷酷的暴风雪
在我命运不远的前方降临

别了，洒满阳光的童年
别了，阴暗的暴风雨的青春
如今已到了在灯红酒绿中
死死地坚守住清贫的年份

自甘淡泊，耐得住寂寞
苦苦不懈地纸笔耕耘
收获了丰富的精神食粮后
荒野上留下个诗人的孤坟

但现在这颗心还没有死
也不是我的最后的呻吟
这不就是生涯的午后吗？
还远远不到日落的时候！

IN THE AFTERNOON OF MY LIFE'S WORK

The winter sun is slowly setting in the west
Yet it is still warm, and even more pleasant than usual
When one feels the accomplishments of the afternoon
Who cares how grueling and depressing the morning was

As winter's setting sun remains gentle
Densely dark clouds gather at the edge of the sky
There is little question that a frigid snowstorm
Is fast approaching

I bid farewell to my sunlit childhood
I bid farewell to the dark storms of my youth
Now in this age of feasting and revelry
I still stick firmly to my plain life

Prepared to live in obscurity, and always content with solitude
I've kept weeding and plowing with my pen
After harvesting riches for the mind
The only grave for the poet left in the wilderness

Yet this heart has not yet reached its end
This is not my final groan
For is this not just the afternoon of my life?
There is still a long time before the sun sets!

September 1–February 18, 1998

中国这地方……

许多令人惊叹的传奇
在这里早已习以为常
连历代王朝兴衰成败
也成小调在民间传唱

古战场出土的刀剑已经冰凉
留下的诗文却令人热血满腔
千百年悲壮史上屈死的英魂
给中华儿女无穷的精神力量

朝霞似火映大好山河
这里创造着太多的辉煌
夕阳滴血涂抹昆仑
这里也留下太多的悲凉

饱览沧桑但却精于世故
历尽艰辛可又不失善良
中国人的秉性如此叫外人不解
中国这地方是这样地令世人神往

 **CHINA, SUCH A PLACE...**

So many astonishing legends
Have long been common here
As even the rise and fall of past dynasties
Are now no more than folksongs sung by the masses

The sword unearthed from an ancient battlefield is already cold
But the ancient poems left to us still warm our blood
Just as the passing of heroic spirits a thousand years before
Offers the Chinese people eternal spiritual power

As if aflame, the mountains and streams illuminated by the morning
    sun
Appear as a brilliant light
Yet the setting sun pours crimson down upon the Kunlun Mountains
Where boundless grief has been left behind

From the wide angle of transience yet always sophisticated
Having endured suffering yet never having lost its gentle nature
It is for this reason that the essence of Chineseness cannot be
    grasped by others
Yet the whole world has always been drawn to this place, China

1998

暴风雪

一

哦，下雪了，正当我在
纷纷扬扬的大雪中独自徘徊
亲爱的，你像一阵风裹着的雪团
砰的一声扑进了我的胸怀

哦，亲爱的，你不再是个女孩
连鬓角也被无情的岁月染白
可茫茫风雪中，我猛然发现
你重现了年轻时身披婚纱的风采

人生就是场感情的暴风雪
我从诗情画意中走来

二

凛冽的暴风雪中冻僵的手指扳动着
车轮的辐条，移动着历史的轮胎
大汗淋漓，耗尽青春的年华
前进的距离却是寸寸相挨

抬头风雪漫漫，脚下白雪皑皑
小风吹过，哆嗦得叫你说不出话来
可要生存就得在苦寒中继续抗争
这就是孕育着精神的冰和雪的年代

人生就是场冷酷的暴风雪
我从冰天雪地中走来

 **SNOWSTORM**

I

Oh, it is snowing as I
Wander alone into the drifting flurries
My love, you are snow wrapped by the wind
Rushing into my chest

My love, no longer a girl,
Your temples have whitened with the years
But in the endless snow I suddenly see
You still looking like a young bride in her wedding dress

Life is just a snowstorm of emotions
I want to walk in an ideal landscape

II

In the snowstorm, frozen fingers turn
Spokes and move the wheel of history
Though sweat drips and youth is exhausted
The distance ahead is still measured in inches

Snow falls endlessly from above while
Ices freezes white from below
Shivering in the wind, you can barely speak
But you must strive to survive the bitter cold
This is the age of ice and snow to incubate the spirit

Life is just a snowstorm of cruelty
I feel like walking in this ice and snow

November 1998–January 1999

世纪末的中国诗人

生就了一副建安风骨
是吃得了苦的灵气书生
脚踏黄土，学贯中西
几千年血缘浑然天成

年轻时曾付出十分惨痛的代价
到中年作出难以想象的牺牲
谁知又遇上一场前所未有的
利己与私欲大作的暴雨狂风

那就让该熄灭的成为灰烬
该吹散的就不留她的踪影
而我却在苦寒之中
精心守护着艺术的火种

添加些我们无用的尸骨做干柴
经寒冬的狂风一吹便大火熊熊
在物欲漫天的冬夜，火焰被吹得
像民族精神的旗帜迎风抖动

化苦难的生活为艺术的神奇
净化被金钱异化了的灵魂
如此我便没有虚度
自幼追求艺术的一生

CHINESE POETS AT THE END OF THE CENTURY

Born with the vigor of the Jian'an style*
I am a gifted scholar able to endure suffering
Standing upon the yellow earth with knowledge of East and West
My nature is conditioned by a lineage spanning thousands of years

I paid a higher price than I should have in youth
And made unimaginable sacrifices in middle age
But I never expected that I would encounter such a wild storm
A torrential downpour of selfishness and material greed

Then let the past fall into ash
And disperse without a trace in the wind
But I still hold onto a cold and simple life
To gingerly protect the tender kindling of art

Toss our useless bones into its fire
And let the winds of winter blow them into flame
In the winter night of materialism
Its flame is like a flag of national spirit, lashing in the wind

Transform this cold life into the majesty of art
Refine the spirit alienated by money
If you do, perhaps I did not waste
These years, this lifelong pursuit of art

1999

---

* The Jian'an style refers to the reign title of Emperor Liu Xie of the Eastern Han
Dynasty, who was in power from A.D. 196 to 220. The poems of this period are
characterized by their political and aesthetic power. Its greatest writers would usu-
ally include "the Three Caos," "the Seven Scholars of Jian'an," and Cai Yan.

青春逝去不复返

只一味执著地追求不知深浅
曾一度陷入无知和偏见的泥潭
到实在无力拔出脚来的时候
才体验到困境绝望与求生的情感

由此对人生百态的感叹
随着青春逝去不复返

人生长河中水呛得死去活来
灌了一肚子操娘的胡骂乱怨
世风日下中逆着浑水浊浪
幸运地闯过了恶运的激流险滩

那健康野蛮的激情朝气
随着青春逝去不复返

到两鬓秋霜，步履蹒跚
月波下细将岁月清点
还真得倒抽一口凉气
好个"高处不胜寒"

可矫健身姿，满头黑发
随着青春逝去不复返……

PASSING YOUTH NEVER RETURNS

Blindly pursuing my goal without knowing its depth
I fell into the mire of ignorance and prejudice
And not until I was unable to pull out my feet
Did I finally experience despair and the will to survive it

Yet after this, the sigh of life's rise and fall
Fell away with youth and did not return

Strangled, half dead, by the long river of life
Saturated in endless fucking abuse
As things are only getting worse, I must walk against its muddy
    current
Fortunately I made it through the turbulent rivers and lethal shoals
    of destiny

But the healthy, wild passions and vitality
Faded away with my youth and will not return

When I began to limp, the hair at my temples turning gray,
I counted my days under the frosty wave of the moonlight
Took a deep cold breath
And admitted that I "cannot bear the chill of the summit"

The agile body, the black hair
Faded away with my youth and will never return . . .

April 27, 2000

相聚

菜盘摞叠起来的酒宴丰盛
不知怎地忆起小时候的情景
大家围坐的偌大的桌上只有
几个空酒杯, 一支啤酒升, 孤零零

喝着生啤酒, 吸着劣质烟
议论着各自莫测的前程
在动荡不安的青春时代
看人生, 未来迷雾重重

几个空酒杯, 一支啤酒升
烟雾中弥漫着浓浓的友情
女友, 斗殴, 家庭的不幸
都哪里去了?——已成梦境

又回到朋友欢聚的酒宴
杯盘狼藉, 醉意蒙眬
添了些时兴的酒肉声色
少了点当年的血气真诚

☀ A GATHERING

As the dishes piled up in an abundant meal
I am not sure why I flashed back to my childhood
Everyone was sitting together around a large table
With only a few empty wine glasses and a lonely pitcher of beer on top

Drinking draft beer and smoking cheap cigarettes
We talked about our uncertain futures
When we lived through those turbulent years
Our futures looked like a heavy wall of clouds

Only a few empty glasses and a lonely pitcher of beer remained
The smoke was filled with the thick bonds between friends
Girlfriends, fistfights, family tragedies
Where has all this gone?—fading into a dream

Come back to the joyful gathering of friends
As the dishes pile up, we get more and more drunk
And the conversation turns to wine, food, songs, and women
But the vigor and sincerity of those days can no longer be felt

July 2000

我的梦

带着胜利者得意的笑容
我边舔着嘴角边的血腥
边盘旋于蓝天俯视着大地——
一只刚刚吃饱了的老鹰

终日相伴烈日，暴雨狂风
暴风雪三番五次逼我至绝境
老天给了我残忍强悍的性格
这是艰难险恶中求生的本能

生来就习惯大自然中的孤独与冷漠
空寂中处处是弱肉强食的野性
一辈子自由自在，独往独来
天地间对我来说是路路畅通

此时，乌云聚集，天空阴冷
我突然想去天外探个究竟
决心不甘平庸，超越自我
来一次不寻常的直线向上的飞行

于是，我鼓动双翅
双脚拼命地乱蹬
踩着无形的天梯
垂直地攀爬天空——

——只要还有一丝气力
　　我就向上，我就不停
　　没劲了，挺住，再来一次
　　妈的，拼了——直到最终

完全耗尽了我的全部精力
我突然改变姿势，来个"倒栽葱"
头朝下，双眼紧闭，双翅夹拢
自高空下坠，耳边是呼呼的风声

快速下落时的刺激令人兴奋
拼死奋挣后又享受身心的放松
激动地我真想大声叫喊
我人生的境界已到了更高的一层

 **MY DREAM**

Wearing the smirk of a victor
I lick the blood from the corners of my beak
Spiraling in the sky looking down upon Mother Earth
An eagle having just eaten its fill

All day I accompany the burning sun or torrential rains and gales
Again and again snowstorms force me into hopeless situations
Still the heavens have given me a hardened resolve
Survival instincts in the face of dangers

Since birth I have grown accustomed to nature's solitude and
    indifference
Though the universe is ruled by the savage laws of the jungle
All my life I have been free to wander the world alone
Heaven and earth have opened for me all of their doors

And now the sky grows cold as dark clouds gather
Suddenly I want to explore what lies beyond the blue
Determined not to be ordinary, I want to surpass myself
To ascend straight up at an angle rarely seen

So I beat my wings
Both feet struggle to stretch outward
I climb the intangible ladder to heaven
A pure vertical line rising past the sky

—So long as I have an ounce of strength
    I will climb without stopping
    Exhausted, I straighten up and start again
    Damn it, I will fight it out—to the very last

I have nothing left
Suddenly, turning upside down
I fall forward end over end
My head plummeting downward, eyes closed, wings pulled in tight
Plunging descent, wind ripping past my ears

The fall, its sheer speed, is exhilarating
After struggling, I enjoy the loosening of body and mind
Ecstatic, I want to call out
I have broken through to another level of consciousness

快接近地面时，我展开双翼
又开始了稳健的水平滑行
可心中还琢磨着刚才的起落
滋味像百感交集的人生

乌云间风声越来越紧
一声霹雳，地裂天崩——
醒来方知是粗茶淡饭后
伏在书案上做的一个梦

As I fast approach the earth, I open my wings
To glide evenly once more
Yet I still think about that rise and fall
Which contains the flavors of life's multitudinous feelings

Within the darkening clouds, the winds still howl and howl
Thunder nearly splits the earth and shatters the sky
Waking up, I realize that I have only been dreaming
Bent over my desk after tea and a simple meal

First draft, 2002/final version, March 7, 2003

解冻的心潮

——听施特劳斯 "春之声"

随着艺术家的手指在琴弦上跳跃
春光在哗哗作响的水面上喧嚣
读着五线谱上神妙的音符
请听我心中阵阵解冻的心潮

春天来了，春天来了
春风醉醺醺地在原野上奔跑
阳光下纯洁的白雪公主
已融入黄土地焦渴的怀抱

回想起福利院严冬阴冷的早晨
这阳光照不到的地方寒气逼人
被轰出被窝的病人袖手缩脖
一件件不合体的衣服紧箍着全身

呵斥声中洗漱间一片忙乱
冰凉刺骨的冷水脏兮兮的毛巾
因怕冷病人的洗漱敷衍了事
就这样冷水还刺痛了我残损的牙龈

难过的还数福利院寒冬的夜晚
呼呼的北风中一片死气沉沉
服药后的病人早早被赶进了被窝
护士则缩在大衣里打不起精神

病房中是躲都躲不开的低级取乐
打骂中夹杂的惨叫更令人寒心
恐惧中暗暗祈盼春天的临近
我终于走出了福利院冰冷的铁门

春天来了，春天来了
春风醉醺醺地在原野上奔跑
阳光下纯洁的白雪公主
已融入黄土地焦渴的怀抱

随着艺术家的手指在琴弦上跳跃
春光在哗哗作响的水面上喧嚣
读着五线谱上神妙的音符
请听我心中阵阵解冻的心潮

THAWING TIDE OF EMOTION

—Listening to Strauss's Voices of Spring

In the wake of an artist's fingers leaping across strings
Spring's landscape flows upon babbling water
Reading astonishing notes on the staff
Please listen to my thawing tides of emotion

Spring is here, spring has arrived
Its wind rushes drunkenly across the open fields
Beneath the sun, the pure white snow
Has already melted into the thirsty breast of the yellow earth

Recalling the bleak winter mornings in the mental asylum
I still felt the pressing cold of this sunless place
Patients driven off their beds, their hands drawn up into their
        sleeves and their necks pulled in
With their ill-fitting clothes tightly binding their bodies

Hurried by the shouting attendants, there was chaos in the bathroom
The bone-chilling water and filthy towels
Tortured by the cold, the patients never really get clean
The freezing water hurt my mutilated gums

There was nothing worse than cold winter nights in the mental asylum
Dead silence inside, the howling wind outside
After forced pills, patients were driven early into their beds
Depressed nurses slouched forward in their overcoats

In the sickroom, vulgarities are unavoidable
Beatings and scoldings joined patients' screams to chill me through
In this despair I'd secretly pray for spring's approach
Finally I walked out through the cold iron gate of the mental institution

Spring is here, spring has arrived
Its wind rushes drunkenly across the open fields
Beneath the sun, the pure white snow
Has already melted into the thirsty chest of the yellow earth

In the wake of an artist's fingers leaping across the strings
Spring's landscape flows upon babbling water
Reading astonishing notes on the staff
Please listen to my thawing tides of emotion

First draft, 2002/final version, March 15, 2003

诗神来了

伴着心跳，你来了，似相约如期
黑暗中我俩的目光不期而遇
可意会不可言传的舒心一笑
就彼此坦白了心中所有的秘密

不知怎的，我这个时代的宠儿
每当感情遭遇风雪之际
就会碰到你这个打小的知己
陪我一起在雪夜里踱来踱去

竟然兴奋地不知你何时离去
因为我专心地在圣洁的雪地上寻觅
辨认着我俩杂乱无章的足印
我认定，这就是流芳千古的诗句

THE GOD OF POETRY HAS COME

With my heart beating, you come right on time
Our eyes meet in the dark by chance
A small smile means more than it can tell
And we reveal to one another our most hidden things

I, the beloved child of the times, do not know why
When my senses fall into the wind and snow
I meet you, my closest lifelong companion
As we wander together into the winter night

I am so excited that I fail to notice you have left
I feverishly search the snowy ground
For our confused footprints
But then it dawns on me that these were poems that would last forever

June 27, 2003, midnight

精神的驿站

终于理清了难以梳理的思绪
用红笔明白地勾出了思考的要点
放下笔,喝口已经凉了的清茶
满意地也是很得意地点起一支烟

搏击了历史和现实的壮阔波澜
在感情剧烈起伏后终于靠岸
脱了缰的思想一夜马不停蹄
现缓缓进入精神放松的驿站

随手关上台灯 推开玻璃窗
外面是天亮前后的半明半暗
深深吸口气活动下僵硬的躯体
分明感到一股黎明时的轻寒

掐灭烫手的烟头,躺在床上
睡意中翻个身稍感有点酸懒
头脑中还在斟酌那只言片语——
该记下来,可实在睁不开双眼……

等明天吧
等到明天
明天……
……清闲

WAYSTATION OF THE SPIRIT

At last I sorted through my puzzled thoughts
Clearly marked the important ones with red ink
All this put aside, I sipped a small cup of cold tea
And lit up a cigarette, satisfied . . . even a little proud

After struggling against the great waves of history
And undergoing the acute rise and fall of feelings, I pulled to the shore
My thoughts ran like an untrammeled horse through the night
And approached the waystation of the spirit's release

I turn off the lamp, open the window
Outside daybreak creeps forward in half-light
Breathing deeply, I move my stiff limbs
Clearly there is, if only faint, a chill before dawn

Putting out the cigarette burning between my fingers
I turn over on the bed, aching, exhausted
Still mulling words and phrases over and over again
I should write them down but cannot open my eyes

I can wait until tomorrow
Until tomorrow
Tomorrow . . .
. . . I will have time

July 19–26, 2003

冬日的阳光

——给寒乐

你是否感受到了冬日的阳光
我可早已嗅到了她的芬芳
在经烘烤变暖的新鲜空气里
在吸足了阳光后略带糊味的衣被上

你可注意到冬天阳光的颜色
浅浅白白地加上稍许的鹅黄
哈气成冰的季节里就这点暖色调
透着严寒中人们的祈盼和希望

可得好好珍惜这暖暖的冬阳
外出走走,享受下这难得的时光
让阳光晒出的好心情随鸽群放飞
鸽铃声牵带出心中的笑声朗朗

淡淡的冬日的阳光不躁动不张狂
独坐在家中品杯茶是乐事一桩
悠闲清静中不妨读几页书
累了,便合上书本,闭目遐想

"冬天到了,春天还会远吗?"
品味着诗句微微睁开双眼
发觉暖暖的淡淡的冬日的阳光
正在缓缓地移出朝南的门窗

SUNLIGHT OF WINTER

—For Han Le

Have you felt the sunlight of winter?
I have already sensed her fragrance
In this warm air, freshly baked
In the slightly burned smells of sun-soaked clothes and sheets

Have you noticed the color of winter sunlight?
Pale white with a touch of light yellow
These are the only warm tones in the season of frozen breath
Revealing in the bitter cold everyone's hopes and desires

Please cherish the warm winter sun
Take a stroll outside, enjoy this rare moment
Let your joy at the sun's warmth fly off with a flock of pigeons
Where the sounds of their bells draw out the laughter in your heart

The pale winter sun isn't restless or arrogant
To sit at home and savor a cup of tea is truly a pleasure
Quietly resting, why not read a few pages of a book
When tired, close the book, then your eyes, and let your thoughts
    roam

"If winter comes, can spring be far behind?"
Savor the verse, then open, slightly, both eyes
Finally, discover that winter's pale warm light
Is migrating slowly out of the southern window

2003

啊，尼采

十九世纪最后的圣诞夜很冷
狂暴的风雪从门缝窗隙挤进了
哲学教授们聚会的金色大厅——
知识界的废话，空话正赢得掌声

略感寒意的教授们皱了皱眉头
夫人们不觉下意识地整了整衣领
谁也没予以理睬，没有反应
可窗外这呼啸的声音
正横扫欧洲上空

门窗外是尼采徘徊踯躅于荒郊
是他的思想在伴着风雪和狼嚎
冰天雪地里他思想一次次地蜕皮
像一次次血淋淋地挣脱精神的镣铐

他在一生中从未停止过追求
没人能理解他性情的孤僻和高傲
也没人回答他对世俗的嘲讽
陪伴他的只有雪片般的手稿

疾病的折磨使他十分苍老
尼采苦苦地在孤独的冥想中煎熬
不安分的思想像狂风裹挟着大雪
席卷天地，狂暴而又肆虐——
一个多么纯洁又残酷的世界

这时敲响了新世纪到来的钟声
尼采所召唤的一代"超人"英雄
从杰克·伦敦笔下的"马丁·伊登"
到和海明威一起打渔的老人
如今已使全世界为之震惊

多少不眠夜中忍受着疾病的折磨
孤独冷漠中怀着诗意的憧憬
思想的婴儿经受了分娩的苦痛
终于喊出了惊天动地的哭声

 OH, NIETZSCHE

The last Christmas Eve of the nineteenth century was very cold
Piercing winds and snow stuffed themselves into the cracks of every
    door and window
As professors of philosophy gathered in the Golden Hall
Their nonsense and hollow academic jargon were winning applause

Feeling a chill, professors furrowed their brows
And refined ladies unconsciously pulled their collars closed
No one paid attention to the chill, no one even responded
But the howling wind outside the window
Swept across Europe's wide sky

Outside, Nietzsche was wandering around in the wilderness
His thoughts were accompanied by the snowy winds and howls of
    wolves
In this frozen world his thoughts shed their skin again and again
Like a bloody struggle to be free of incorporeal chains

He relentlessly pursued the truth
No one could understand his eccentric and arrogant disposition
No one could answer his disdain for this world
For only a blizzard of manuscripts accompanied him

Weathered by a tormenting disease
Nietzsche bitterly suffered from his solitary meditation
His discontent with thoughts surged like gales blowing the heavy
    snow
Sweeping the sky and earth with a wild fervor
What a pure yet brutal world

At that moment the bells of a new century were ringing
The generation of heroes Nietzsche called "supermen"
From "Martin Eden" penned by Jack London
To the old man who went fishing with Hemingway
Have already shocked the whole world

Through so many sleepless nights he endured the torture of disease
Yet nurtured the poetic longing of solitude and indifference
An infant thought undergoes the trauma of birth
To finally cry out in an earth-shattering voice

尼采，当改变世界的太阳到来前
满天迸发闪烁着你思想的火花
快熄灭的烛火燃烧着你最后的激情
尼采啊尼采，让我们一路同行

Nietzsche, before the sunrise changed the world
The entire sky shimmered with your incandescent thoughts
The nearly extinguished candle was burning your final passion
Nietzsche, oh Nietzsche, let us walk on together

(2003)

五十多岁了

入夜，老伴为我沏好一杯茶
在床头灯下把纸笔靠枕放好
斜倚在床上我随意点上一支烟
让思想天马行空般脱缰野跑……

……五十多岁了 到五十多岁
才发觉生活这样美好……

记得中学时冬夜也沏杯酽茶
多多地放上糖然后在灯下苦熬
困得实在不行了，就灌上几口
让又苦又甜的茶水在心头猛浇

那时拼命吮吸着知识的乳汁
还是一棵正茁壮成长的幼苗

文革间政治风云变幻无常
"红太阳"烤得一身汗口干舌燥
"经风雨"又淋得从头一直湿到脚
整天地患"政治感冒"昏头昏脑

灵魂已被触及得哆里哆嗦
早就失去了自我可谁都不知道

之后精神病院里唯唯诺诺
病房里不是打架就是争吵
为点烟，沏茶甚至为看新闻
不得不低三下四地向护士讨好

一直无奈地在人前装着笑
没一点做人的尊严与自豪

入夜，老伴为我沏好一杯茶
在床头灯下把纸笔靠枕放好
斜倚在床上我随意点上一支烟
让思想天马行空般脱缰野跑……

……五十多岁了 到五十多岁
才发觉生活这样美好……

156

OVER FIFTY

As night falls, my wife steeps a cup of tea for me
Placing a pen and paper beside the pillow under the bed lamp
I recline on the bed and casually light up a cigarette
Letting my wild thoughts rise limitless, like celestial horses running
    across the sky . . .

. . . More than 50 years old—It has taken me this long
To see how beautiful life can be . . .

I remember brewing strong tea during high school's winter nights
Pouring sugar in, I labored under the desk lamp
When I began to drift off, I would drink even more
Letting its pungent sweetness and bitterness stir my mind

Then I sucked in the milk of knowledge with everything I had
For I was still a sapling waiting to grow

During the Cultural Revolution, politics changed incessantly
The "Red Sun" scorched us, leaving us sweaty and thirsty
Sent out to the countryside to "Experience Wind and Rain," we
    were soaked to the bone
As we succumbed to a "political influenza" through our days

Tortured, our spirits shivered
We had already lost ourselves, but no one knew it

Thereafter I became a submissive coward in a mental institution
In the psych ward fistfights and arguments often broke out
To get smokes, tea, or even a newspaper
I had to suck up to the nurses with saccharine flattery

I was forced to smile in public
Having lost the last of my dignity and pride

As night falls, my wife steeps a cup of tea for me
Placing pen and paper beside the pillow under the bed lamp
I recline on the bed and casually light up a cigarette
Letting my wild thoughts rise limitless, like celestial horses running
    across the sky

. . . More than fifty years old—it has taken me this long
To see how beautiful life can be . . .

June 24–26, 2004

我的歌声

在漫长的冬季, 在冰天雪地之中
我匍匐在地, 身上是厚厚的冰层
在见不到阳光的地方低声歌唱
心中在暗暗地祈盼着大地的解冻

这凄美动人的故事已成传说
那含泪的诗句读来娓娓动听

谁知春寒后又是近三十个苦夏
我伤过, 死过在屈辱中求生
我心的原野在一番刀耕火种后
又经铁锄一次次残忍的修整

留下的诗篇字字醒目狰狞
字句间气味带着汗臭血腥

不料辉煌的秋收后万物凋零
又一场私欲膨胀的恶雨狂风
当诗歌不再纯净而失去了听众
孤寂的秋风中仍飘荡着我的歌声

一边歌唱, 一边老泪纵横
这回惊动四座的是嘶哑的喉咙……

 ## MY SINGING

In the endless winter, a world of snow and ice
I crawled along the ground, a thick layer of ice covering me
I whispered songs in a place where no sun can be seen
Secretly, my heart prayed for the earth to thaw

This moving story has become legend
A poem filled with tears sounds so poignant when read

Who could have known that thirty harsh summers would follow the
    spring's chill
I was injured and almost died; I shamelessly begged for life
The field of my mind was slashed and burned
Then was brutally exhumed by iron hoes again and again

Each word I have left in my poems is strikingly hideous
The smell of sweat and blood rises from between them

Who could have known that all things withered after the autumn
    harvest
And even now the wild winds of another greed-swollen storm
    approach
When poems lose their purity, they lose their readers
My songs still drift through the lonely autumn wind

I sing as tears run down my aged face
This time it is my hoarse voice that shocks those who listen . . .

July 23, 2004, Dongjuan [a residential area in the
Baiwanzhuang neighborhood of Beijing]

秋雨

不知何时起窗外秋雨淅沥
当我在窗前穿衣看到了这一幕:
秋叶像老人一样,在秋雨中哆嗦着
在做落叶归根前最后的清洗

我冷到了心里,索性躺到床上
不觉想到也该梳理下自己
清点自己思想的庄稼地里
有多少成熟的果实并一一采撷

从发现问题到一步步深入地解析
饱满的精神粮食一颗颗一粒粒
聚集在一起像原野上的红高粱穗子
风雨中我观点鲜明地举起了火炬

发展中出现的新因素使研究向前继续
像秋雨要几经冷暖才融成点点滴滴
又从高空跌落,滋润秋播后的大地
才最后化造出孕育明年丰收的神奇

一切就这样悄悄地进行
默默地但有序地交接更替
在淅淅沥沥的秋雨声中
思想的天空一点点地清晰

天空终于放晴了?! 我忙起身
推开窗子,舒心地长出一口气
只见秋雨后的树叶又现生机
颤巍巍地点头表示: 还算满意

☀ AUTUMN RAIN

Unaware that a soft autumn rain had begun to fall
I stood before the window and saw
Autumn leaves like old men shivering in the rain
Before returning to their roots, this is their final shower

Chilled to the core, I lay back in bed
Feeling the need to clear my head
To take stock of my orchard of thoughts
How much fruit hangs ripe that I may pick them one by one

First the finding, then the solving, one problem at a time
In one grain, then another, spiritual sustenance is found
Gathered together like red sorghum ears in the fields
I raise a torch, bright even in the wind and rain

Newly developing elements push inquiry further
Just as the autumn rain, after endlessly freezing, melts into drops
And falls from heaven to moisten the earth after autumn's seeding
Creating the miracle born of next year's harvest

This all happens so quietly, so secretly
Silently recycling each other in a balanced order
Through the continuous percussion of autumn rain
The sky of thoughts slowly begins to clear

The sky finally clears up?! I quickly rise
And open the window to take in a long releasing breath
I can see the leaves reviving after the autumn rain
Still quivering, they nod, somewhat satisfied

October 3, 2004

观《卢昂大教堂》有感

我们不得不惊叹莫奈的敏感，
他所捕捉的是再普通不过的景象——
夏日常有的"白花花"的正午的阳光，
直射在卢昂大教堂的白色大理石上。

可以想象莫奈顶着烈日酷暑，
眯着眼睛，在卢昂大教堂边徘徊徜徉，
可怎么也想不出他怎样在阴暗的画室里
天才地把这"刺眼"的阳光移到了画布上。

UPON SEEING "ROUEN CATHEDRAL"

We have to marvel at Monet's sensitivity
What he paints could not be more ordinary—
Summer's white noon sunlight
Shining directly upon Rouen Cathedral's white marble walls

I can imagine that Monet under this intense sun and heat
Narrowing his eyes, wandered and lingered about Rouen Cathedral
But I cannot fathom how in his dark studio
He so brilliantly transported that glaring sun onto his canvas

October 19, 2004, Baiwanzhuang [a neighborhood in Beijing]

苦夏

这颗悬在半空的心呵
正像这丰收在即的麦田
因为生长着太多的希望
也就牵带出多种的悬念
　　　　——题记

就怕下雨，麦子烂在地里边
毁了大半年的辛勤，大半年的血汗。
当带雨意的风一吹，心就悬了空，
紧紧锁住的眉头难得舒展。

盼着晴天，赶快把麦子收完，
可金灿灿的麦田一眼都望不到边。
地头上还能有大树绿荫的庇护，
麦芒上的太阳可火辣辣地烤人烫脸。

一肚子的"心思"想找朋友分担，
可原野一望无际，亲朋遥远。
只得一个人顶着冒火的太阳
弯着腰一下下地收割一点点地向前……

这场苦夏心灵的收获，
是使我的心受尽煎熬。
愁得我几夜就两鬓斑白，
心绪起伏却诗意昂然……

经历了这场"心灵夏收"的孤独
是什么成了我心中最大的企盼———
就盼着这颗悬在半空中的心呵，
能够稳稳当当地落回地面。

我想大概在丰收成定局的秋天，
到那时，我的歌会少些忧郁和伤感，
因浸透着瓜果的香气和晶莹的秋露
歌声将更香甜，更纯净，更饱满，更沉甸甸！

BITTER SUMMER

Ah, this heart that hangs in mid-sky
Is like a wheat field just before harvest
Growing full of potential
It gives rise to so much suspense

—a note for the title

I am frightened that too much rain would rot the wheat lying in the
field
Would destroy a year of hard work, blood, and sweat
When the wind hints at more rain like an empty heart hanging in
the air
My tensed brow cannot relax

I am looking forward to clear skies, to finally harvesting the wheat
Yet these golden fields seem endless to me
The long shadows of trees shelter the edge of the fields
Yet above the wheat, the burning sun broils the fieldworkers' faces

My mind overflows with ideas to share with friends
But the fields look endless, and my friends and family are distant
Having no choice but to endure the burning sun
I bend over, reaping gradually and moving slowly

The harvest of my soul in this bitter summer
Tortures my heart
Grief whitens my hair at the temples
My mind rises and falls but is laden with poetry . . .

After experiencing the solitude of "the summer harvest of my soul"
I finally come to know what my mind desires the most—
I only hope that my heart, hanging in mid-air,
Might one day land safely once more

When the harvest is finished in the autumn
My songs will not be as melancholy and sentimental
Because they will be soaked in autumnal fruit and crystal dew
My songs will be sweeter, purer, fuller, and heavier than ever before!

July 2, 2005, Shang Zhuang [a neighborhood in Beijing]

远离尘嚣

远离尘嚣，远离人间的烦忧，
有什么能比心灵纯净些更好。
早起，沏好一杯茶，点燃一支烟，
让整个心随茶叶烟缕缓缓飘摇……

白天躲开都市车水马龙的喧闹，
在乡下静得可以听见自己的心跳；
神闲气定地阅读自己喜爱的文章，
过去，未来，比较分析中冷静思考。

夜晚，避开酒吧那灯红酒绿的繁华，
在村舍关上灯能见窗外星光闪耀，
静下心来，试想乘上弯月的扁舟
驶向夜空，渐入梦境，一宿的好觉……

远离红尘中人头攒动的场合，
免得引发扰乱心境的浮躁；
既挣开名缰利锁的精神羁绊，
也摆脱尘世无休止的牵挂与操劳。

放开则让心在空气清新的郊外，
小马驹似的由着性子撒欢野跑；
静下来则如一潭深不见底的湖水，
风吹过，只几沦涟漪，不起波涛……

FAR FROM THE FRENZIED CROWD

Far from the frenzied crowd, and far from the conflicts of the
mundane world
Nothing can be better than a pure spirit
Rise early, brew tea, light up a cigarette
Let your whole heart sway with the sinking tea leaves and rising smoke

Avoiding the noise of city traffic by day
I can hear my pulse in the solitude of the countryside
I can read my favorite literature with a peaceful mind
And silently meditate on things past and that may be

Evading the lively market of bars by night
I can see the bright stars shining outside the cottage window when I
turn off the lamp
Slowing my mind, I imagine stowing away on the skiff of the
crescent moon
Driving deep into the dark sky, I enter a landscape of dreams and
sleep through the night

Keeping far from the crowded spaces of society
For fear of thoughtless distractions
By doing so, I can not only break free of the spiritual bind of vanity
But also cast off the endless worry and strain of the earthly world

Releasing my mind into the pure air outside
I let it run like a wild colt
Calming down, my mind becomes a measureless lake
As the winds blow, there are only a few circles of ripples, but no
waves . . .

First draft, October 20, 2005/final version, November 14, 2005

家

五十多岁才有的家
——给寒乐

雪夜归来，开了门，家中暖融融
拉开灯，光线很柔和，心头一明
拍打去身上的积雪，脱掉外衣裤
感到外衣罩裤上寒气很重

老伴忙着用电热壶烧开水
我感到冻僵的脚趾尖火辣辣地有点疼
但换上在家穿的棉靴后，很宽松
走了几步，点上烟，才在沙发上坐定

直到水壶有了甜滋滋的响声
觉身上发热，我想脸一定通红
夹烟的冰凉的指尖有点发痒
暖意使疲惫的我，一动都不想动

水烧开了，老伴为我沏好茶
我专注着茶叶在杯中起伏飘零
心随叶片一片一片地沉下去
房间内只有钟表答答的响声……

多好的心灵滋养和体力康复
我深感到劳累后彻底的放松
掐灭烫手的烟头，喝上一口茶
从里到外，透着自在从容

已不再记得寒风中的瑟瑟发抖
也不回想雪夜里的摸索独行
暖暖的家中品着茶，却分明在听
窗外一阵阵呼啸而过的寒风

HOME

The home I finally found in my fifties
—for Han Le

Walking back through a snowy night, opening the door, home is
    warm
Turning on the lights, a mild glow appears and my heart becomes
    luminous
Brushing off the snow, peeling off the outer layers
Their heavy chill bleeds through

My wife quickly boils water in an electric kettle
I feel my toes aching and burning
But feel relaxed and comfortable easing into a pair of simple cotton
    slippers
Walking a few steps, I light up another cigarette and move to the couch

The teapot whistles
I'm finally warm; my face must be aglow
My cold fingers tap my cigarette, as if itching
And warmth roots me here; I don't want to move an inch

After the water is boiled, my wife makes tea for me
And I lose myself watching the leaves rising and floating
My heart gently unfurls and sinks with the leaves one after another
Inside the room, only the clocks sound their hushed ticks . . .

How wonderful it is to nourish the soul and restore the body
Absorbed by a relaxation that can only follow exhaustion
I put out the burning cigarette and take a sip of tea
As a deep calm spreads throughout

I don't remember shivering in the cold wind
Nor do I recall groping through the dark, wintry night alone
Savoring the tea in my warm home, I can clearly hear
The cold wind howling outside the windows

First draft, May 18, 2006, 1:18–1:35 A.M./
final version, May 27, 2006, 3:00–4:34 A.M.

春 雪?

天气预报: 立春已过十多日, 但今夜可
能还有一次降雪过程, 雪量不大。

天黑黑的很阴,
夜风不冷但湿漉漉的
想必是细碎的春雪已悄然降临
屋内暖气很热
便敞开了窗子
潮润润的空气便立刻浸漫了身心

关上灯, 漆黑一片, 什么都看不见
但外面在落雪却分明感到很真
有了, 这正是艺术追寻的"感觉"
说不清道不明的, 让人回味不尽

暝暝中突然觉得二千多年来
生命力极强的中国诗学的须根
正沿血脉在我被春雪裹着的
暖暖的心中缓缓地向外延伸

没有一点痛苦的感觉
倒有点从未有过的亢奋
有点酒后微醉的得意
心境却大海般平静又深沉……

随着这根须的伸展, 我仿佛听到
从远古传来的讲授诗学的声音……
赶紧把几天来纷杂的所思所悟
整理成诗句记在这午夜时分

之后可能是两种结果:
第二天早晨醒来, 忙起身
昨夜下了雪, 外面窗台上
薄薄一层, 白白的, 很均匀……

还有一种可能:
第二天醒来, 忙起身
昨夜无雪, 天很阴……

 **SPRING SNOW?**

Weather forecast: Spring began more than ten days ago
But tonight there may be some snow, yet not heavy

Dark, an overcast sky
Night winds blow, not cold, but damp
Spring's light snow must already have been falling
The central heating has made it too hot inside
So the window is opened wide
And moist air quickly floods my body and mind

Turn off the lights, it's pitch black, I can't see anything
But the snow falling outside feels very real
Yes this, right now, is what art pursues, this very "feeling"
That lingers beyond cognition, yet raises endless thinking

In the dark, I suddenly feel the last two thousand years
The vitality and strength of Chinese poetry, its fibrous root,
Running along my veins to my heart wrapped in spring snow
And slowly extending outward

Not feeling any pain
On the contrary, I have never been so excited
As if intoxicated
Yet my mind feels as peaceful and deep as an ocean . . .

As the root hairs stretch, I seem to hear
From a remote history a voice offering an ancient poetics . . .
In a hurry, I begin to untangle these confused thoughts and ideas
Into verses, and write them down this very midnight

Afterward, there are only two possibilities
I wake in the morning
Last night's snow lies on the windowsill
A thin layer, white and even . . .

Or, perhaps, the other possibility:
I wake in the morning
Last night no snow fell, only an overcast sky . . .

(2006)

# TO MY AMERICAN READERS

Shi Zhi

It is morning. Sitting in a small wood near my residence in a Beijing suburb, I spread out a sheet of paper on the cardboard resting on my knees and begin to write these notes.

It is early autumn now. Warm sunshine falls through leaves and branches and illuminates sections of the meadow below. The grass has not yet turned yellow. This is Beijing's best season.

I love nature, I love freedom, but I love poetry even more. The tough experiences that I went through have shaped me. Because of my dismal fate, I had little choice but to take pen in hand to write out the grief that lies at my center so that I might achieve something of an inner equilibrium. For more than thirty years I have been called a lunatic, and I have spent twelve years since the 1990s in an insane asylum, where I lost all of my personal freedom. During that time, it was poetry and a heart cultivated by poetry that saved my life.

I learned to write poetry in 1965 (if not earlier). My poems then—for instance, the first poem of "Ocean Trilogy"—were immature yet tender and simple, and I actually still like them.

When the Cultural Revolution started in 1966, like many young students I lost any semblance of reason and normalcy. Only a heart cultivated by literature since childhood enabled me to object to or, in situations where objecting was impossible, avoid getting caught up in the most extreme inhuman acts. By the end of that year, the Red Guards had been disbanded, and the once-conceited small suns had become counterrevolutionaries.[1] The young middle-school students who had been Red Guards soon rejected all forms of social activism and turned their attention to

---

1. Translator's note: Red Guards were students and other young people in China who were mobilized by Mao Zedong as a political policing force in 1966 and 1967 during the Cultural Revolution. These groups quickly spread throughout China but were soon disbanded because of their increasingly violent and destructive behavior, which plunged the nation into near-chaos.

drinking, smoking, losing themselves in infatuations, or reading, thinking, or debating other topics. This was my generation.

The enormous psychological collapse generated by these historical circumstances combined with a poetic mind led me to write more than ten poems during that period. The dominant theme of the time was the feeling of being disoriented and confused but unwilling to sink into obscurity. These works included "Ocean Trilogy," "Destiny," "Fish Trilogy," "Smoke," "Wine," "Believe in the Future," and "This Is Beijing at 4:08." Handwritten copies of these poems spread widely among youth because they happened to express the feelings of the Red Guard generation. To have witnessed my poems being read widely throughout society is perhaps the thing I am most proud of in my life.

However, misfortune soon followed. After I was demobilized from the army because I could not understand things that were happening around me—I might even go so far as to say that I no longer knew what was happening at all, and others could no longer understand my words or actions—I was sent to a mental hospital on November 25, 1973. It was a very painful time in my life, yet it was only the beginning. I wrote a few poems during this period, two actually: "Pain" and "The Spirit, Part Two" (written in October 1974).

This, then, was how it started . The Cultural Revolution ended, and because of the aforementioned historical background and my insistence on some of my own ideas, I became a frequent visitor in mental institutions.

After the Cultural Revolution, China began a period of Opening Up and Reform and began talking about human rights; all the while, I was furious about the unfair treatment I had received. My poems " Love Life," "Mad Dog," "My Heart," "The Poet's Laurel," and many others were written at this time.

After that, my mind was thrust into even deeper agony, and I was sent to the Beijing No. 3 Welfare House in the suburbs of Beijing to begin my twelve-year period of isolation in an insane asylum. There, the severity, lack of freedom, and isolation stood in sharp contrast to the rise of the market economy and the growth of material desires in the outside world. I wrote "The Final Return," "Life Stages," "Eight Years in a Psychiatric Ward," "In the Afternoon of My Life's Work," "Chinese Poets at the End of the Century," "This Is How I Write My Songs," and "Passing Youth Never Returns." Composing these poems was a long intellectual journey filled with great pain and joy that sustained me through these difficult years.

The situation finally took a favorable turn. On March 21, 2002, a kind-hearted, intelligent woman who loves my poetry (and who is now my wife) made a resolute decision and rescued me from the mental institution.

It has been more than five years since I came out of the mental hospital. I have started to live the life of a normal man. The simple, free, and peaceful life that I now lead has yielded works such as "Sunlight of Winter," "Home," "Autumn Sun," "Autumn Rain," "Celebrations of Autumn Harvest," "Far from the Frenzied Crowd," "Oh, Nietzsche," and "Spring Snow?"

When we speak of poetry, we naturally think of temperament and spirit. Poetry is the sigh a human heart makes at the unfolding of its fate. I write about my own fate, but I have always loved the works of M. Lermontov,[2] some of whose poems are sighs at his fate. It is a pity that his life was so short, as this limited the number of poems he could compose about his fate. He did not write to the end.

I have to mention one thing: the education I received from childhood was in the idealist tradition of Soviet-Russian ideology, which claims that poetry is a clarion call, or poems are bombs and banners. This line of thought also appears in some of my poems, including "Nanjing Bridge over the Yangtze River" and "Our Generation."

What I want to point out specifically is that since I left the hospital, life has been quiet and easy. With a now-peaceful mind, I came to embrace the tradition of classical Chinese poetry: to savor the flavor of life in tranquility. After reading some theoretical articles, especially those by Fu Xinying 傅新营 from the Shanghai Academy of Social Sciences Publishing House, I learned how to savor flavor, which is a special aesthetic frame of mind formed in the history of the Chinese people. It is a very sophisticated way to appreciate the peculiar feeling of art (non-Chinese artists are feeling and pursuing this, too). So some changes have taken place in my more recent poems, such as "Sunlight of Winter," "Home," "Autumn Sun," "Far from the Frenzied Crowd," and "Spring Snow?"

I went home for a simple lunch at noon and a short rest, but I have now come back to this wood to continue writing. This small wood, bathed in the afternoon sun, has become a natural oxygen bar. The singing of cicadas is the only voice.

---

2. Mikhail Yuryevich Lermontov (1814–1841), a highly influential Russian romantic writer and poet who is not well known in the West but who is often compared to Shelley.

Next I want to talk about my opinion of the United States and American culture, and also say something about Chinese culture and the current world we all inhabit.

As early as the Mao period, when I was still a junior high school student, I borrowed Dreiser's *Trilogy of Desire*. At that time in China, the movie *Store of the Lins* was playing. Boss Lin, naïve yet cunning, was a businessman who ran a small store; he was nothing like Frank Cowperwood, the protagonist of *The Financier* (the first novel in the trilogy), who was also a businessman. Cowperwood was willing to take risks in order to make more money, and he ended up getting thrown in jail; after he was released, he participated in the reconstruction of Chicago following the great fire of 1871 and went on to became a financial tycoon. I was amazed by his bravery, wittiness, and ambition, but I could not help feeling from that early moment on that Americans and Chinese are very different from one another. The scene from Cowperwood's childhood in which he watched big fish eating small fish and small fish eating shrimp remains vivid to this day.

Later I read such American writers as Jack London, Hemingway, and Updike, from whom I came to understand the scientific mind and the spirit of intrepid figures. Their steady composure and broad vision left a great impression on me.

I felt that American culture is the culture of the strong. Extraordinary courage and charm lie in sharp contrast to Chinese culture, which I think of as being more temperate, kind, courteous, restrained, and magnanimous. All of these qualities make the power of American culture more concrete and tangible. I have also long thought of American culture as being largely generated by the young. Full of youthful vitality, they are not inhibited by the restrictive effects of tradition; they go their own way without reservations, writing about whatever they encounter, solving any question that might happen to come up. It is indeed lively and joyful, if a little reckless. But the United States is so strong that I do believe it will continue to mature.

It is not like Chinese culture, which has a lot of reservations, which hesitates and stammers when talking about things. But the Chinese regard their culture as something very precious. They look at it again and again, touch it, feel it, and end up loving it all the more. Yet as to the sufferance of the Chinese and their habitual attitude of forbearance, little was mentioned in classical works. In the poem "The Old Charcoal Seller" by the Tang poet Po Qu-yi, there is the line "But though his coat is thin he hopes for winter—Cold weather will keep the price of fuel high." Yet there are few other lines like this one, and the suffering of the people can hardly be found in their folklore.

Now I would like to share something regarding what I find most profound about Chinese culture. The Chinese analyze problems from the six directions: north, south, east, west, up, and down. They look at problems from the standpoint of the living environment of human beings, the earth, and the universe. Of course, this perspective emerged with the eventual enlargement of the horizon of the Chinese people. The way of the Chinese people's thinking is that of a realization, a consideration of various factors about heaven, earth, and humans within the six directions. The philosophy is a bit like the Indian way of Buddhist meditation, through which one comes to a conclusion.

On the contrary, the Western way of thinking expands along a more linear path: the more they think, the finer and more sophisticated their thoughts become.

I do not know whether you are still following my meaning, but if you are, let me ask a question: What was Einstein's way of thinking? I think he combined the Eastern and Western approaches, which would be to synthesize (from multiple vectors or directions) as well as to achieve a realization of various scientific achievements gained through sophisticated linear thinking, which in combination led to his extraordinary findings. Of course, this is just a thought; I am not sure whether I am right.

What is more, Chinese culture is very capable of absorbing elements from other cultures and rarely rejects other cultures. Before Indian Buddhism was spread to China, this was written of the Chinese people:

> Yin and Yang quickly shift,
> Like morning dew they always pass
> Life itself moves so quick
> Unlike gold, life will not last
> Rulers are always replaced in time,
> Sages, they, too, cannot last.
> Nothing is better than drinking good wine,
> No dresses more comfortable than those of silk design.[3]

---

3. I chose to translate these passages with an attention to sound, but for a previously published translation of the "Nineteen Ancient Poems," see Tony Barnstone and Chou Ping, eds., *The Anchor Book of Chinese Poetry: From Ancient to Contemporary* (New York: Anchor Books, 2002), 35.

Even the Grand Councilor Cao Cao (of the Eastern Han Dynasty) wrote of sighing: "Here before us, wine and song / Will life be short or long? / Like morning's dew, / Bitterness prevails as days are few."[4] They knew only about the present life and the present transient world. But after Indian Buddhism was introduced, the Chinese people learned about previous lives and the worlds that follow this one. Then there were such verses written as "Who was the first to see the moon over the river bank, / When did the moon first shine upon man early in the day?"[5] and "When will the moon be clear and bright? / With a cup of wine I ask the blue sky,"[6] all of which questioned the universe after thoughtful meditation. Indian Buddhism witnessed several ups and downs in China over more than 1,000 years, from the Eastern Han Dynasty (206 B.C. to A.D. 220) to the Northern Song Dynasty (A.D. 960 to 1127), and was finally absorbed by Chinese culture and became part of Chinese civilization. Here I recall something that the late Chinese female writer Bing Xin said in her later years: "When will Mr. Democracy and Mr. Science settle in China?"[7] I wish heartily to perpetuate this second exchange of Chinese and Western culture, the first one being the May Fourth movement in 1919.

Finally, the cohesive nature of Chinese culture is something worthy of comment. There are many stories about famous mountains and rivers in China that are passed down from generation to generation. It might be as small as a story passed down orally by one family or village. There is one story about the family with the surname "Mou" in the southeast of Shandong Province. Their ancestors came from the region of Mongolia and did not originally have a Chinese surname. What could they do? Then a cow suddenly made a noise. The family elder said, "Let our surname be 'Mou.'" I heard this story from a friend who had heard it from his mother, who was from Shandong and whose surname was "Mou." In another such example, in the place where Jiangsu, Anhui, and Shandong provinces meet are two counties called Feng and Pei. Throughout history, only people from those two counties could use yellow cloth to bundle items for carrying; historically in China, the royal family were the only ones who could use the color bright yellow. This special privilege was allowed because these two counties were the place where Liu Bang, emperor of the Han Dynasty, incited his insurgence. People in this

---

4. This is a famous poem attributed to Cao Cao, one of the central figures in *The Three Kingdoms*, simply titled "Short Song Style." This is my translation.
5. Zhang Ruoxu, A.D. 660–720, a poet of the Tang Dynasty.
6. Su Shi, A.D. 1037–1101, a poet of the Song Dynasty.
7. Bing Xin (1900–1999), a famous Chinese contemporary writer.

region could recognize those from Feng or Pei by the yellow color of their bundling cloth. Stories such as these are spread within clans or across certain regions; they undoubtedly function as a tie to connect families and regions and provide a great cohesive force in nations and countries. "From the wide angle of transience yet always sophisticated / Having endured suffering yet never having lost its gentle nature,"[8] they know everything about history but are extremely discreet in life and afraid of government officials—terribly afraid. They never dare talk or behave recklessly. As they develop discretion from experience, they learn to speak differently to different people out of self-protection. Thus it is not difficult to understand why Chinese people and Chinese culture emphasize knowing right from wrong.

After China introduced the policies of Opening Up and Reform, accompanied by economic improvements, people believed that their lives were getting better. Because "the biggest mistake is education"—the words of Deng Xiaoping 邓小平 upon his 1989 resignation—the Chinese people have gained weight but are less strong in spirit; they have become smarter but are less honest; they may have more money, but they have less of a sense of responsibility for the nation and society.

Has China truly lost its spirit, though? No, not really. I want to tell you about something I recently experienced. It was November of 2002 when I got out of the hospital. My wife and I were invited to a poetry conference in Guangzhou. The day we traveled there on the train happened to be my birthday. We were traveling with our old friends, the poet Hei Dachun 黑大春 and the Dutch sinologist Maghiel van Crevel. There were new faces, too: two young poet-musicians, Shui Yuan 水原 and Le Shou 乐手. Because it was my birthday, people toasted me during dinner, and I got to know these young artists.

The second day, still traveling, we talked. As is customary, I asked about their lives. The several young men who were floating in Beijing said they had no support from their families and led the irregular, unguaranteed life of vagrant artists. Their only means of supporting themselves was through performing, which wasn't much—200 yuan [about $30] for each performance. Some hosts included a free meal and some did not. Their life was hard. When they did not perform, some of them ate only one meal a day. Even colds were something they could not afford, which made morning exercises necessary even in winter. But they never lost their love of art.

---

8. From Shi Zhi's poem "China, Such a Place . . ."

Because of my experience (which they knew about), I could not help but ask, "The ancient people said 'the misfortune of the nation is the fortune of the poets.' What do you think of this?" To my surprise, these young artists answered me unanimously, "Of course it is better when the nation is fortunate!" Tears welled up in my eyes. How they reminded me of myself when I was young!

This is the heart and soul of these bold, bizarrely dressed artists who are considered the hardest to control by those in power, who are labeled "problem youth" by society. Their determined pursuit of art, their admiration for their national art, and their love of their nation and people surpass everything. The true reason why Chinese culture can live forever and be passed down from generation to generation lies here. The reason the Chinese people do not die lies here.

Some people say that China is in great disarray right now. I would rather say that it is simply very dynamic. The Chinese people have just started to be able to experience their "selves," so why would they not want to express themselves a little? After thousands of years of feudal autocracy, young people (up to middle age) are finally able to express themselves individually without breaking the law. Yet we have to admit that the degree to which we are seeing a clash of ideas is unprecedented. This is a sign of the rejuvenation and reconstruction of the Chinese culture. This is a very encouraging dynamic phenomenon and something that everyone is debating.

As I finished these notes, perhaps it was the will of heaven that a gust of wind blew through, making the leaves of white poplars in the woods rustle. It was very quiet. I held my breath and listened to the sound of nature itself. It sounded like barely audible laughter from heaven, or perhaps from the bottom of my heart.

September 12, 2007, 3 P.M.
Finished in the small wood by Xiyu River in Beijiao, Beijing, China

Translated by Jonathan Stalling

# TRANSLATOR'S ACKNOWLEDGMENTS

I first heard Shi Zhi in 2007, at a poetry reading at the Old Story Bar in Beijing. I was transfixed by the uncanny way the grain of his deep, resonant voice activated the formal elements of his poetry. As he read aloud, his eyes closed, his body slightly swaying, the subtle layering of rhymes and light folk rhythms hovered somewhere between poetry and whispered incantation. In her excellent essay "Guo Lusheng," published in the Zephyr Press collection *Today,* the poet and scholar Cui Weiping quotes Shi Zhi as saying, "You have to have a window, a form; then you can look through it." Listening to Shi Zhi's framed landscapes, we not only see but hear what lies beyond.

Of course, when one translates a poem, the formal nature of this window undergoes inevitable changes. Languages are not transparent glass through which we see the same world; they are first and foremost sounds in time, sounds that shape how and what we come to see, hear, and feel. I have spent years experimenting with ways of mimicking Chinese prosody, yet after trying numerous times to create loosely metered and rhymed English versions of Shi Zhi's work, I eventually abandoned the effort because I could not create a consistent English formalist idiom flexible enough to hold the full semantic weight of his poetry. Words transmit referential meanings, but the sounds they make also hold meanings. You can translate referential meanings with a certain degree of fidelity, but the meanings that arise from the sounds these words make depend on culturally specific ways of hearing, and I do not think one can shake a metered and rhymed version of Shi Zhi's work from the hold of Victorian verse culture, which retains a lock on how we hear formal prosody in English. If Shi Zhi were inspired by Western poetic rhythms, I would not hesitate, but his work's formal elements derive from the folk idioms popularized from the 1930s to the 1960s in China and impart a radical mixture of emotive possibilities ranging from ideologically overdetermined patriotic sounds, to uniquely oral idioms of the countryside. Therefore, I chose to translate these poems into what I hope the reader will find to be lyrically charged free verse able to impart Shi Zhi's voice without interference from the static of the history of English formalism in our ears. While English readers will not have access to the aural textures of Shi Zhi's original poems, something of the feel still emerges here within an English soaked in the singularly mythic dimensions of his poetry. I also take a minimalist approach to punctuation, opting only to use punctuation to disambiguate the English when the Chinese is not equally ambiguous or when the Chinese uses punctuation to signal exclamatory remarks or other unusual phrasing.

I began working on Shi Zhi's poetry in 2006, when I translated a few of his new poems for *World Literature Today*. I then heard him read his work the following year at the Beijing poetry reading, which had been organized by Zhang Qinghua (a fiercely formidable poetry scholar based at Beijing Normal University). Before Shi Zhi performed, I gave a poetics paper, exploring his turn toward the themes of classical Chinese poetics in his post-institution poems. It was after this talk that he gave me all of his poems to translate. Over the last three years, translating Shi Zhi's poetry has become something of a daily practice, a continual return to that strangely kenotic practice of seeking something from the "inside" (my mind/language/experience/sensibilities) that comes from the "outside" (another's mind/language/experience/sensibilities)—a practice of housing someone else and in return finding myself housed within him.

In point of fact, this plurality did not stop with Shi Zhi and me; it continually widened to encompass an ever-growing cast of friends and colleagues who collectively made it possible for the translations in this volume to materialize. I owe a debt of gratitude to many who have offered their kind, wise, and always generous comments, critiques, and suggestions. In particular I would like to thank Zhang Zhe, who, over two intense weeks in 2007, went through every poem with me, disambiguating words and lines, which prepared the way for the English translations, which have matured over many versions and variations over the last four years, benefiting from the generous comments of Yao Benbiao, Jami Proctor-Xu, Liu Qian, Yun Wang, Howard Goldblatt, Wu Yongan, Yun Wang, and finally Christopher Lupke and Afaa Weaver, who have both been critical readers and strong advocates of this work. I will remain forever indebted to Zhang Qinghua for arranging my first meeting with Shi Zhi and for his help in selecting the poems for this volume and writing the introduction to the book. Of course, I need to reserve a special space in these pages to acknowledge the continual companionship of Shi Zhi. We have traveled to Qinghai province together, and spent hours in conversation in hotel rooms, conferences, bars, and classrooms over the last four years discussing these poems and many more topics. He also spent a great deal of time correcting the Chinese versions of the poems collected in this volume, which had heretofore been misprinted in existing Chinese editions (some of his poems exist in several forms due to the fact that so many people memorized them in the late 1960s and early 1970s). This meant that I had to retranslate those revised poems and lines. I have footnoted all the major changes, but I have not indicated where his revisions are merely correcting typos and misprints. Shi Zhi's wife, Han Le, has also been a great help and an angelic presence throughout the translation process.

Finally, I would like to thank Byron Price, Chuck Rankin, and Jay Dew of OU Press; *Chinese Literature Today* assistant editor Julie Shilling; and my brilliant copy editor, Jane Lyle. I would also like to thank my colleagues at Beijing Normal University for their support, especially Dean Zhang Jian, Professor Liu Hongtao, and Professor Zhang Qinghua, who, along with my colleagues at OU, Dean Paul Bell, R. C. Davis, and Ron Schleifer, have made the CLT book series a reality.

These translations also benefited from a grant from the Oklahoma Humanities Council that allowed me to travel to China to meet with Shi Zhi again in 2008. The publication of this book and other volumes in the CLT book series is made possible by a generous grant from the Hanban and the support of both Beijing Normal University's College of Chinese Language and Literature and the University of Oklahoma's College of Arts and Sciences.

And as always, I want to thank my whole family for their support, but especially my immediate family—Amy, Isaac, Eliana, and Rowen—for their continual immersive presence.

Jonathan Stalling